RECLAIMING YOUR SAVAGE

SOVEREIGNTY

WORKBOOK BY
LISA LACY

Reclaiming Your Savage Sovereignty ©2025 Lisa Lacy

Paperback ISBN: 979-8-89704-428-3

Publisher: Double Edge 7

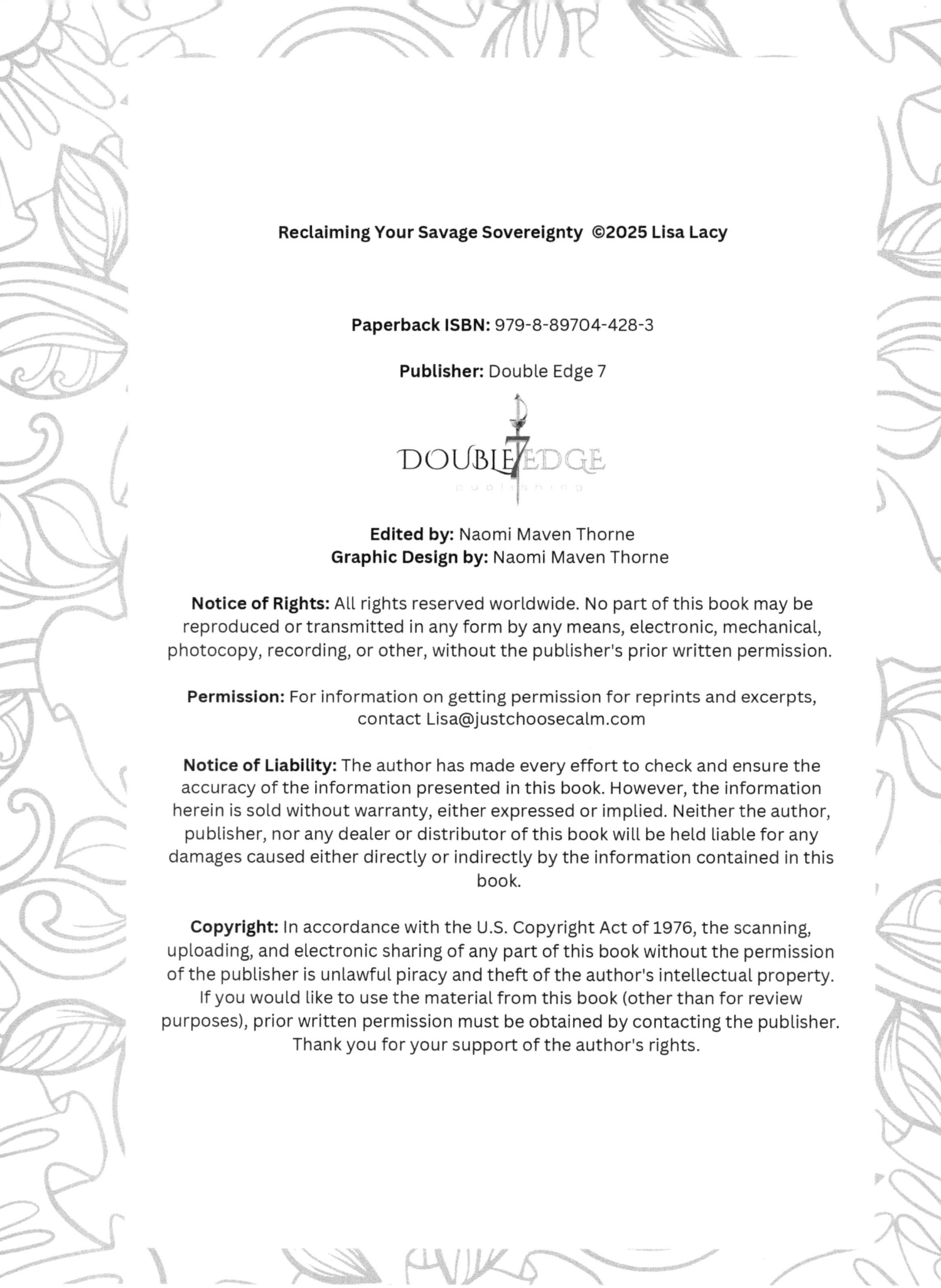

Edited by: Naomi Maven Thorne
Graphic Design by: Naomi Maven Thorne

DEDICATION & GRATITUDE

This book is a battle cry, a reclamation, and a love letter to those who dare to break cycles and reclaim their power. It exists because of the unwavering support, creativity, and presence of some extraordinary souls.

- **To Brody Dudley:** for standing beside me through every wild, audacious idea, never flinching, never doubting, always believing. Your faith in me is an anchor in every storm.

- **To Charlsie Carpenter,** for simply existing. Because sometimes, that alone is enough to change the world.

- **To Lisa Schneider,** for the rare and sacred gift of listening without expectation. Your presence is a sanctuary, and your wisdom ripples further than you know.

- **To Naomi Maven Thorne,** whose creative brilliance and intuitive design make my vision tangible. You speak my language in ways few can.

- **To Mom,** for surviving. For making it through, against all odds, and showing me what resilience truly looks like.

- **To Missy Maxwell-Worton,** my publisher, for being the beacon of belief in an out-of-the-box vision and for daring to take a chance on this radical idea. Your unwavering trust in something unconventional and profound has made it possible for this message to reach those ready to hear it. You've turned the impossible into reality, and for that, I am deeply grateful.

- **To Katy Landis,** for being an incredible accountability partner, pushing me to continue rising like a queen from the ashes. Your unwavering support, guidance, and belief in me have been crucial in helping me keep moving forward even when the path seemed unclear.

- **To my clients,** for stepping outside their comfort zones, for walking the path of healing with courage, and proving that transformation is not only possible, it is inevitable when you choose yourself.

- **And to you,** the ones holding this book, those who continue to do the work. By healing yourself, you heal your lineage. By reclaiming your truth, you shift the vibration of the planet. This path is not easy, but you were never meant to be small.

With gratitude, fire, and relentless love,
Lisa Lacy

XO love

TESTIMONIALS

01

Lisa Lacy is a fierce, insightful Lioness, yet a kind force to reckon with. Her book is not only a guidance method to reclaiming your identity, it is a beautifully, masterfully, and thoughtfully constructed instrument to inspire consciousness and self-worth.

Lisa makes this journey fun through a proven technique where one seeks to find true identity, let go of the past, and develop a personal sense of purpose.

⭐⭐⭐⭐⭐ -ALEXANDRA ASBURY (TRANSFORMATIONAL COACH)

02

"There is nothing more powerful than self-introspection, challenging our own mind and creativity! Lisa Lacy has resourced all three transformative powers in this brilliant workbook. I highly recommend taking your time and moving through these pages, as you will undoubtedly gain far more than you will lose if you don't."

⭐⭐⭐⭐⭐ -SUMMER JEAN, INTEGRATIVE SOUND PSYCHOTHERAPIST

03

THE POWER OF F'OFF: A GUIDE TO RECLAIM SAVAGE SOVEREIGNTY is a truly refreshing guided journey designed to help you celebrate your strengths and recognize your weaknesses. In valuing creativity in this workbook, Lisa uses tools such as coloring exercises to access neural pathways in a way that may not be often accessed in our everyday lives.

The Power of F'off encourages us to be assertive without aggression in situations when we might otherwise be taken advantage of; to stand our ground when our self-esteem is being challenged, and to honor our right to make our own choices when we might otherwise feel guilt.

This work celebrates emotional intelligence and self-love. It challenges activities and those who drain one's energy and empowers taking a stand for one's individuality. All these things to catalyze personal growth!

⭐⭐⭐⭐⭐ - DR. ANDRE WALTON

04

"The Power of F'Off Workbook" feels like having a bold, no-nonsense best friend walking beside you, one who's not afraid to tell it like it is while helping you work through the emotional baggage that's been weighing you down. It's raw, real, and refreshingly honest. The included coloring pages are a fun and thoughtful touch, offering the perfect mental break when the emotional work gets heavy."

⭐⭐⭐⭐⭐ -KRISTINA SIMS GOLDENSOULWI LLC

05

I joined Lisa's course a few months ago, completely broken and hopeless, and ready to give up. I was not sleeping, not eating, and was in pure hell. Those who knew me then would say I had no chance of coming out of it. But the end result? I am happier now than I was ten years ago. I have a passion for life, and I smile constantly. This program is so easy to follow, and it works, pure and simple. It works!

⭐⭐⭐⭐⭐ -ANGELA G. CLIENT

CHAPTERS

Lisa Lacy

LISA LACY

Course Instructor

WELCOME TO MY COURSE

Welcome to **Reclaiming Your Savage Sovereignty.**
You did it. You've arrived here, holding this workbook, standing at the edge of your own transformation.

And let me tell you, this isn't just a book.

This is a movement. A **rebellion against everything** that has tried to keep you small, stuck, and silent.

This is your story, unfolding in real-time.

LISA LACY

About the Author

Lisa Lacy created the **F'Off Method** out of necessity, because healing through silence, shame, and sugarcoated strategies wasn't cutting it. After surviving narcissistic abuse, addiction, complex trauma, and multiple near-death experiences from a rare blood disorder, she realized: healing requires something more radical. Something real.
It requires **sovereignty.**

The **F'Off Method** was born as a battle cry for radical self-love and emotional freedom. It teaches what most systems don't: how to face the truth, own your boundaries, choose yourself without apology, and finally take action that sticks.

C.A.L.M. *or (Conscious Awareness & Liberation Method)*

From that foundation, Lisa developed the **C.A.L.M.** Approach, her signature trauma-informed healing system. **C.A.L.M.** is a soul-led path that reconnects people to their truth, calms the chaos of survival mode, and builds a life anchored in clarity, courage, and conscious choice.

This approach integrates Lisa's groundbreaking 3-part framework:

EIRTA
(Emotional Intelligence for Recovery from Trauma and Addiction)
for cultivating self-regulation and reparenting the wounded self.

CCC
(The Consciousness Cauldron Curriculum)
where shadow work meets spiritual sovereignty and inner alchemy.

ATRT
Advanced Trauma Reprocessing Technique,
a deep healing protocol combining neural rewiring, somatic activation, and energetic clearing

Lisa is a nationally recognized speaker and coach who has spent over 25 years empowering others to rewrite the narrative of victimhood into stories of victory. Her work is a fusion of clinical wisdom, lived experience, and sacred rebellion.

Reclaiming Your Savage Sovereignty is more than a workbook.
It's a mirror.
A match.
A map back to the fire inside you.

Because reclaiming your power isn't about fighting harder.
It's about remembering you never gave it away—you just forgot where to look.

To work with Lisa, message her at: Lisa@justchoosecalm.com

Check out the offerings on the website: justchoosecalm.com

DISCLAIMER

I AM NOT:

A doctor, psychologist, psychiatrist, or other trained medical professional. I am in no way practicing medicine, and aside from my own **personal experience,** I do not claim to have a medical or therapeutic background. I am not a licensed or accredited counselor, nor do I endorse any or all of this program for every person.

 ## I AM:

A survivor of trauma, addiction, mental illness, and near-death experiences, defying all the odds after surviving multiple pulmonary embolisms. My journey through Bipolar Disorder, Borderline Personality Disorder, and Complex PTSD has **forged a path of radical healing.**

 ## THIS IS NOT:

"One size fits all." You will need to tailor this and adapt it for success, and I will teach you how. However, the non-negotiable aspect of this program is simple: **You must show up for yourself, have an open mind, and do the work!** I make no promises, but this program will work for you if you do the work.

THE EXPECTATION:

Not everyone will have success with this program because not everyone will be willing to put in the work. **It will take dedication and a willingness to change.** There is no easy fix or shortcut. You are expected to struggle and even fall but your journey is a lifelong lesson and ultimately worth it!

WHAT THIS COURSE IS

"The Power of F'Off" is more than instruction; it's a guided journey through the trenches of your past, the chaos of the present, and into the sovereignty of your future. You won't just read, you'll engage, interact, and reclaim.

This workbook is a **hybrid of storytelling and self-mastery,** a fusion of my rawest experiences and the exact tools that helped me **break cycles,** heal trauma, and say **F'Off** to everything that no longer served me. This is **your permission slip** to stop playing small, stop explaining yourself, and step fully into your own power. You don't need to be "fixed," **you need to be unleashed.**

Inside, you'll find:

- 01 -

REAL STORIES

Because healing isn't theory, it's **lived experience**.

- 02 -

ACTIONABLE TOOLS

Because transformation requires more than just **awareness.**

- 03 -

INTERACTIVE EXERCISES

Because this isn't about passive learning—it's about **active** reclamation.

THE SACRED COLORING PAGES: A TOOL FOR EXPANSION

Throughout this workbook, you'll notice intricate sacred coloring pages woven into the pages. **These are not just aesthetic additions; they are portals to your subconscious mind and anchors for healing.**

Sacred coloring pages, **inspired by mandalas and ancient geometric symbols,** are tools for mindfulness, healing, and inner expansion. Each page in this workbook serves a unique purpose:

If words start to feel overwhelming, turn to a sacred coloring page for solace. If a **breakthrough** is brewing, let your hands move with it. This isn't just art, **it's alchemy.**

- 01 -

FOCUS & REFLECTION

Use them as visual **meditation tools** before beginning each section.

- 02 -

INTENTIONAL COLORING

Engage with them through art; as you color, breathe into your healing, infusing it with your own **energy.**

- 03 -

ACTIVATION SYMBOLS

Embedded within the designs are patterns that energetically align with the lessons you're about to uncover.

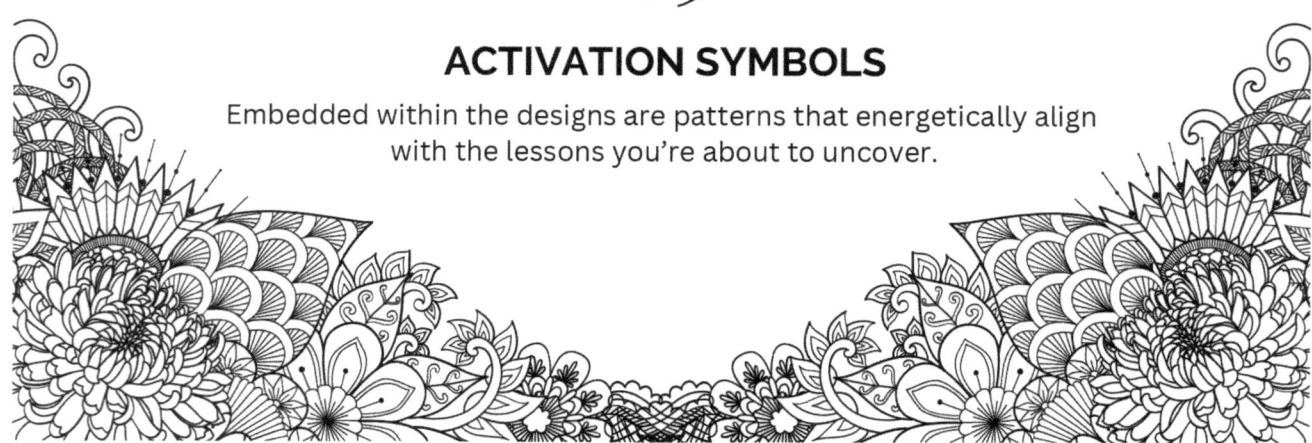

THE SACRED COLORING PAGES: EXAMPLE

You will receive one of these dedicated coloring pages at the conclusion of each chapter, providing you with an opportunity to reflect, process, or take a break. These pages are designed to help ground you or work through moments of resistance.

HOW TO GET THE MOST OUT OF THIS WORKBOOK

- 01 -

ENGAGE WITH THE EXERCISES

Don't just read; write, reflect, and let it all out.
There are pages provided to allow you to meditate.

- 02 -

GIVE YOURSELF SPACE

Some lessons **will hit deep.** That's good. Honor your process.

- 03 -

EMBODY THE F'OFF ENERGY

This isn't about perfection. **This is about reclamation.**

- 04 -

RETURN TO THE SACRED COLORING PAGES

Let them ground you in moments of resistance.

HOW TO GET THE MOST OUT OF THIS WORKBOOK

This isn't just another self-help workbook. This is a warrior's manual for the ones who refuse to stay small. **For the cycle-breakers, the rebels, the ones who know there's more waiting for them.**

Are you ready to take back what's yours?

Then let's begin.

CHAPTER

01

THE MOMENT EVERYTHING CHANGED

There comes a point when you realize you've had **enough; enough** of people walking all over you, enough bending until you break, and enough swallowing your truth to keep the peace. That moment doesn't come with sirens or dramatic montages. It creeps in like a **slow-burning fire**, fueled by every ignored red flag, every swallowed "no," every moment you let someone else dictate your worth.

And then, one day, it happens.

You're in a conversation, or maybe a confrontation, where someone assumes they own your time, energy, and choices. They toss their expectations at you like you're there to simply carry their weight. Maybe it's a boss who just keeps taking, a friend who only calls when they need something, a partner who drains you, or a family member who weaponizes guilt.

And that's when you hear it.

It rises from **deep within,** unfiltered, absolute, and undeniable. Maybe it's a whisper. Maybe it's a scream. Maybe you don't even say it out loud, but the energy of it surges through you like wildfire, burning down years of conditioning. **"F'OFF."** And just like that, **you are free.**

Not free from responsibilities. Not free from struggle. But **free from the illusion** that you owe your compliance to anyone. **Free from the guilt** that kept you saying "yes" when you should've walked away. **Free from the belief that your worth is measured by how much you tolerate.**

But What Now?

Knowing you need to change is one thing. **Taking back your power is another.**
This is where you master the **F'OFF Framework,** not as an act of rebellion, but as an act of self-respect and radical self-love.

MASTERING THE "F'OFF" METHOD FOR RADICAL SELF-LOVE

01

F – Face the Truth

What is draining you?

Who or what have you been tolerating for too long? **Face it. Name it. Own it.**

Action Step: Write down the relationships, habits, or beliefs that no longer serve you.

You cannot change what you refuse to confront. If you keep excusing toxic people, justifying toxic patterns, or avoiding hard truths, you will stay stuck. **This is your wake-up call.**

02

O – Own Your Boundaries

Emotional intelligence isn't just about understanding feelings; it's about protecting your peace. **You don't need permission to set boundaries**.

Action Step: Decide **ONE** boundary you will set today, whether it's saying "no" to toxic people, breaking a habit, or stopping self-sabotage.

Owning your boundaries isn't about shutting people out; it's about **choosing yourself** over the expectations that suffocate you.

03

F – Fully Choose Yourself

Radical self-love means choosing **YOU** every single day. **It's not selfish, it's necessary.** No one is coming to save you.

Action Step: Say this out loud: **"I choose myself. I am no longer available for what drains me."** Feel the shift in your energy.

Choosing yourself means no longer making excuses for those who treat you like an afterthought. **It means walking away without looking back.**

04

F – Fearlessly Take Action

Saying "F'Off" is only powerful if you back it up with action. You don't need a perfect plan, you just need to **take the first step.**

Action Step: Take immediate action, block the number, leave the situation, apply for that job, and start therapy. Whatever it is, **do it NOW.**

Every time you take action, you prove to yourself that you are **not stuck. You are not powerless. You are not obligated to tolerate what depletes you.**

MASTERING THE F'OFF METHOD

Action Step: Write down the relationships, habits, or beliefs that no longer serve you. **What is the ONE boundary you will set today?**

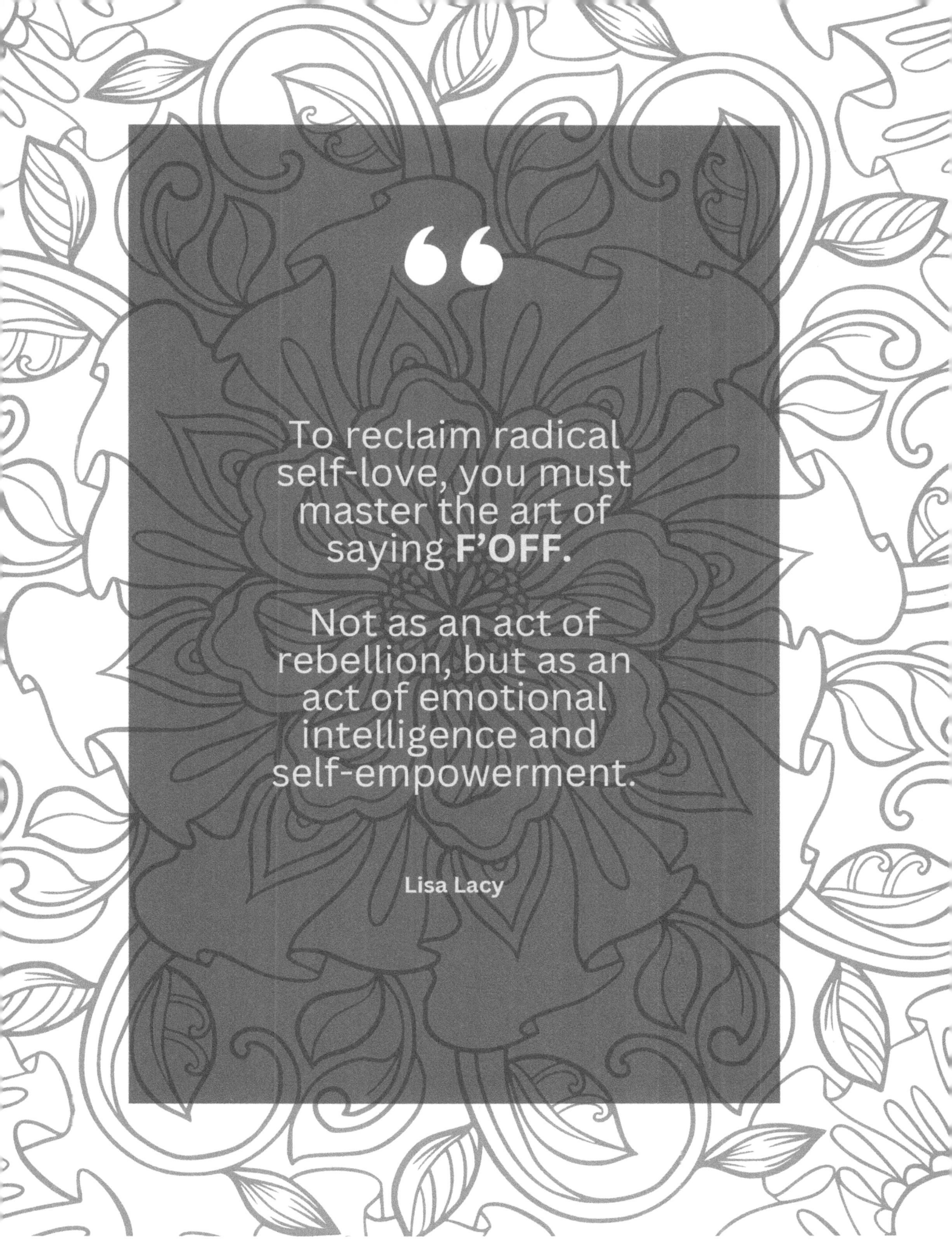

> "
>
> To reclaim radical self-love, you must master the art of saying **F'OFF.**
>
> Not as an act of rebellion, but as an act of emotional intelligence and self-empowerment.
>
> Lisa Lacy

THE MYTH OF BEING "NICE"

The biggest scam of all time?

The idea that being **nice** means being **passive.** We're told from childhood:

- Be nice.
- Be polite.
- Be agreeable.
- Don't make waves.

Girls are taught to be accommodating. Boys are taught to suppress their emotions. Employees are trained to be obedient. Society grooms us to keep our heads down, smile, and say nothing.

But being nice should never mean being a doormat. Being kind doesn't mean being spineless. Being understanding doesn't mean tolerating the intolerable.
You can be kind and still have boundaries.
You can be compassionate and still demand respect.
You can love someone and still tell them, **"F'OFF,"** when they cross a line.

THE ART OF SAYING F'OFF (WITH STYLE)

Saying **F'OFF** doesn't always mean shouting it in someone's face (though sometimes that's exactly what's needed). There are many ways to master the art of firmly, unapologetically reclaiming your space.

01

The Silent F'OFF

You don't owe anybody an argument.

You don't owe anyone an explanation. Sometimes the most powerful **F'OFF** is simply walking away. **Unfollow. Block. Ignore.** Let them talk to the version of you that no longer exists.

02

The Polite F'OFF

Some situations call for grace.

A simple, "I appreciate your perspective, but I'm going to do what's best for me," is a beautifully passive-aggressive way of telling someone to mind their own business.

03

The Direct F'OFF

Sometimes, people need to hear it plain and simple:

- "No. That doesn't work for me."
- "I'm not available for this conversation."
- "I won't tolerate being spoken to like that."
- Each of these is a professional way of saying, **"F'OFF"** with a smile.

04

The Energetic F'OFF

Not everyone deserves your reaction.

Some people thrive on your frustration, your attention, your energy. The greatest power move? **Refusing to engage.** Nothing confuses a manipulator more than a calm, disinterested exit.

THE REVOLUTION STARTS NOW

This is your awakening.

This is where you stop explaining, over-giving, and making yourself small. It's time to **unapologetically reclaim your peace, and your life.**

- You don't need permission.
- You don't need approval.
- You just need the power to say, **F'OFF**.

And that power? **You've had it all along.**

- Every time you say "no" to something that drains you, you are saying yes to yourself.
- Every time you refuse to shrink, you take up the space you were meant to occupy.
- Every time you unapologetically protect your peace, you win.

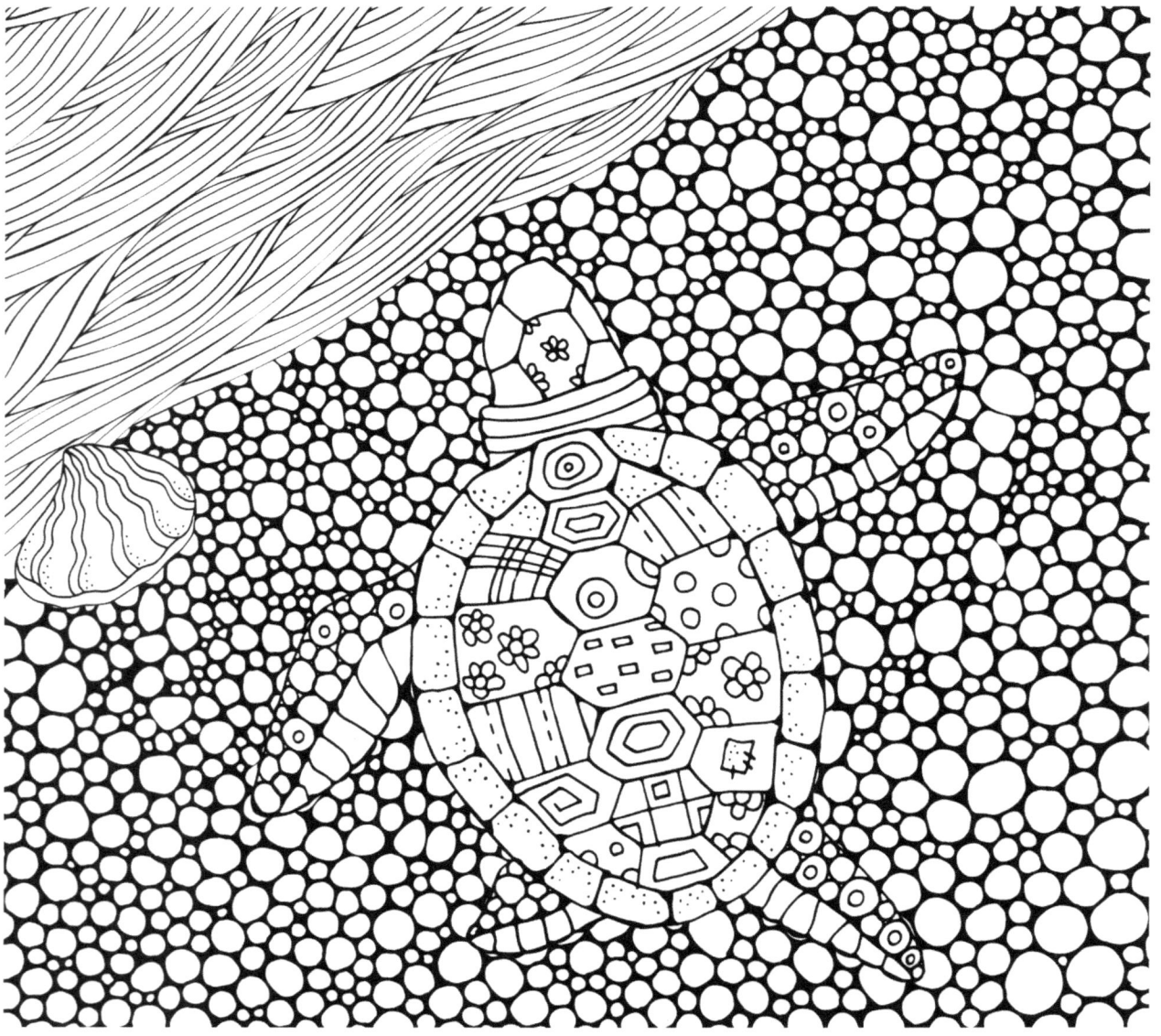

SMALL RITUALS TO START OWNING YOUR POWER

- 01 -

THE MIRROR MOMENT

Every morning, look yourself in the mirror and say:
"I do not owe my peace to anyone. My boundaries are sacred."

- 02 -

DAILY BOUNDARY CHECK-IN

Take a few minutes each day to reflect:
Where did I say "yes" when I meant "no"?
Awareness is the first step toward change.

- 03 -

THE F'OFF JOURNAL

Start a journal where you write down one thing each day that you are **no longer tolerating.** Watch how much **power you reclaim.**

- 04 -

F'OFF

This is where it begins.
This is where you rise.
This is where you say, with
**full conviction
F'OFF.**

I WILL NO LONGER TOLERATE

Action Step: Start a journal where you write down one thing each day that you are no longer tolerating. Watch how much power you reclaim.

REFLECTION QUESTIONS: WHAT DOES THE WORD "SOVEREIGNTY" MEAN TO YOU?

HOW DOES IT FEEL TO CLAIM FULL OWNERSHIP OVER YOUR CHOICES, EMOTIONS, AND BOUNDARIES?

WHAT EMOTIONS HAVE YOU BEEN SUPPRESSING TO KEEP THE PEACE OR MAINTAIN THE STATUS QUO?

REFLECTION QUESTIONS: WHAT DOES THE WORD "SOVEREIGNTY" MEAN TO YOU?

WHEN WAS THE LAST TIME YOU SET A BOUNDARY AND HELD IT? IF IT'S BEEN A WHILE, WHAT STOPPED YOU? IF YOU HAVE, HOW DID IT FEEL?

WHAT IS ONE SMALL BUT RADICAL ACT OF SELF-SOVEREIGNTY YOU CAN COMMIT TO TODAY? HOW WILL IT SHIFT YOUR ENERGY MOVING FORWARD?

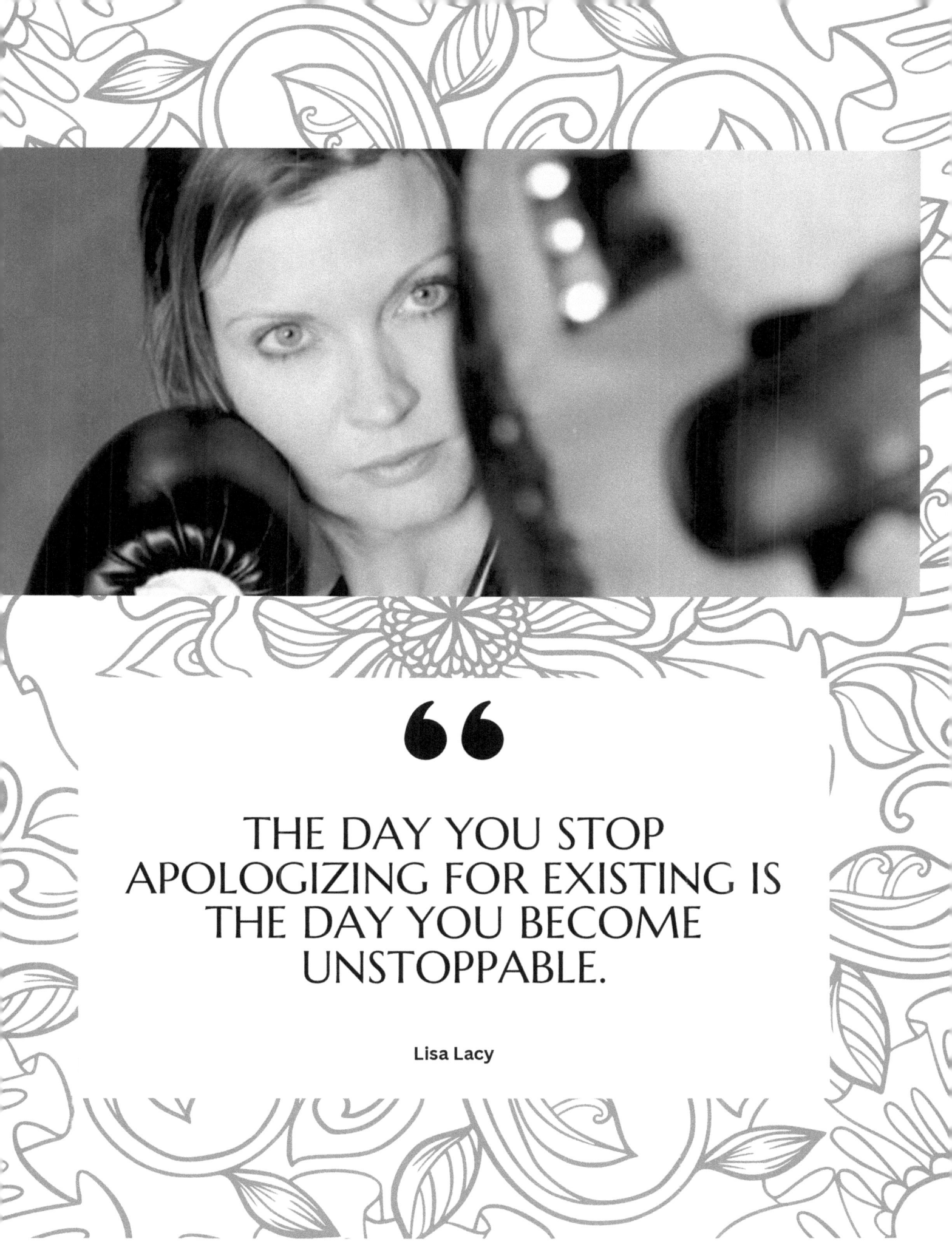

THE DAY YOU STOP APOLOGIZING FOR EXISTING IS THE DAY YOU BECOME UNSTOPPABLE.

Lisa Lacy

FINAL THOUGHT

The Power of F'OFF as a Daily Practice

Saying **F'OFF** isn't just a one-time event. It's a daily practice of choosing yourself over fear, manipulation, and expectations.

CHAPTER

02

——

BORROWED TIME
LIVING WITH PULMONARY
EMBOLISMS

The Moment That Stopped Time

The first time I had a **pulmonary embolism**, I thought I was dying. The last time? **I knew** I was. There's a distinct sensation that comes with having a blood clot block your lungs. It's not just the pain, it's the weight of it. A **crushing force**, like invisible hands squeezing the breath out of your body, reminding you just how **fragile** you really are. It's a mix of suffocation and panic, where every inhale is a battle, and every exhale feels like it could be your last.

Most people don't survive one pulmonary embolism. **I have survived many.**
Some might call that **resilience.** Others might call it **luck.** But when you live with **hereditary antithrombin III deficiency**, survival isn't just about chance; **it's a war against your own blood.**

A Life Written in Blood

I was born with a **genetic disorder** that affects only about **0.02%** of the population. A flaw in the very thing that keeps me alive, **my blood.** Antithrombin III deficiency makes my body more prone to forming dangerous clots, even when there's no injury.

I don't need a catastrophic accident or surgery for my blood to betray me; it happens on an ordinary Tuesday, when I'm sipping coffee or walking across a room. **My own body is constantly working against me**, trying to shut me down like a machine with a **wiring defect** that no one can fully repair.

EVERY DECISION CARRIES RISK:

- Can I sit for too long?
- Will this flight cause a clot?
- Did I take my blood thinners **exactly** on time today?

Because even the smallest **misstep** can mean the difference between **another day alive** and **another trip to the ER,** if I even make it in time.

Pulmonary embolisms don't wait for you to be ready. They strike like **assassins**, silent and sudden, turning a normal moment into the **brink of death.** And for me, that brink is a place I've visited **far too often.**

THE UNWANTED MILESTONE

It happened again.

I knew the signs before they even fully settled in: a tightness in my chest, a creeping shortness of breath, an all-too-familiar dizziness. At this point, **I don't need a doctor** to tell me when my blood has decided to **play Russian Roulette.**

The problem is, **PTSD doesn't let me go to the hospital without a fight.** When you've survived **medical trauma** over and over, hospitals stop feeling like places of healing and start feeling like a **war zone.** The fluorescent lights, the smell of antiseptic, the cold metal of the IV stand, it all screams **"Danger!"** to my nervous system. My body remembers **every** needle, every moment of teetering between this world and whatever comes next.

So, instead of doing what a rational person should do, **going to the ER immediately, I** hesitated. I rationalized.

"Maybe it's not that bad this time."
"Maybe I can sleep it off."
"Maybe, just maybe, my body will let this one slide."

But my body doesn't negotiate. By the time I arrived at the hospital, I was on the edge of losing consciousness. I don't remember the exact moment I passed out, but I do remember waking up to the beeping of monitors, an oxygen mask pressed to my face, and a doctor standing over me with the kind of look that people wear when they've seen **death and barely pulled someone back from it.**

"You're lucky to be alive," he said. I wanted to tell him that **luck had nothing to do with it.** But I was far too busy catching my breath.

THE WEIGHT OF BORROWED TIME

The hardest part of surviving isn't the **moment of crisis,** it's the **aftermath.** Waking up and realizing that, once again, you've **cheated death**. It's the quiet reckoning with the fact that **you shouldn't be here,** but somehow, **you still are.**

And that realization is both a gift and a curse.

Because when you live on **borrowed time**, every moment is magnified, every joy, every regret, every wasted second. There's an urgency to it, a desperate need to make **everything** matter because you never know when **the final embolism will come, the one that you won't survive.**

People love to say, **"Live every day like it's your last."** But what if you've spent years knowing that it could be?

MASTERING THE F'OFF FRAMEWORK TO OVERCOME FEAR

F – FACE THE TRUTH

Action Step: Write down the **biggest fear**
holding you back from fully living.
Is it fear of death? Fear of failure? Fear of time running out? **Confront it.**
What is the reality you've been avoiding?
What fears have kept you stuck?
Face it. Name it. Own it.

MASTERING THE F'OFF FRAMEWORK TO OVERCOME FEAR

O – OWN YOUR BOUNDARIES

Fear thrives in hesitation. Protecting your peace means setting boundaries with **your own thoughts and actions,** not just with other people.
Action Step: Set a boundary with yourself. **No more hesitation. No more negotiating with fear.** Whether it's seeking help sooner or prioritizing joy, **own your decision.**

_____

_____

_____

_____

_____

_____

F – FULLY CHOOSE YOURSELF

I don't get to choose whether or not I have this disorder. But I do get to choose how I respond to it. **And I choose me.**
Action Step: Say this out loud: **"I refuse to live in fear. I choose to be fully present in my life, no matter what."**

F – FEARLESSLY TAKE ACTION

Every moment I delay out of fear is a moment I lose.
And **I don't have time to waste.**
Action Step: Take one immediate action today that moves you toward living fully, whether that's making a bold decision, reaching out for help, or stepping outside of your comfort zone. **Do it now.**

WHAT ACTION WILL I TAKE:

Action Step: Take one immediate action today that moves you toward living fully, whether that's making a bold decision, reaching out for help, or stepping outside of your comfort zone. **Do it now.**

SMALL RITUALS TO EMBRACE LIFE FULLY

- 01 -

THE "I AM ALIVE" LIST

Every night, write down one moment that made you feel truly alive. It could be as small as feeling the sun on your face or as big as a meaningful conversation.

- 02 -

THE BODY GRATITUDE PRACTICE

Instead of resenting your body for what it's been through, place your hands over your heart each morning and say, **"Thank you for keeping me here."**

- 03 -

INTENTIONAL BREATHING

Take 60 seconds a few times a day to **breathe deeply, slowly, and with intention.** It's a small but powerful reminder that **you are still here.**

THE "I AM ALIVE" LIST

Every night, write down one moment that made you feel truly alive.
It could be as small as feeling the sun on your face or as big as a
meaningful conversation.

MINDSET SHIFTS TO OVERCOME FEAR OF MORTALITY

- 01 -

YOU ARE NOT YOUR DIAGNOSIS.

You are the way you choose to live.

- 02 -

EVERY BREATH IS A SECOND CHANCE.

Treat it as such.

- 03 -

YOUR PURPOSE IS NOT TO SIMPLY SURVIVE,

it is to live.

PRACTICAL STEPS TO MAKE EVERY MOMENT MATTER

- 01 -

ELIMINATE TIME-WASTERS

If you knew you had one year left, what would you spend time on?
If it's not a soul, "Yes!", don't do it.

- 02 -

SPEAK YOUR TRUTH NOW

Stop waiting for the perfect moment. **Say what you need to say, now.**

- 03 -

SCHEDULE "JOY" LIKE YOU SCHEDULE WORK

Book time for the things that bring you pleasure.
If you wait until you're "free," you'll never get to them.

REFLECTION QUESTIONS: WHAT WOULD YOU DO WITH BORROWED TIME?

IF YOU KNEW YOU HAD ONE YEAR LEFT, WHAT WOULD YOU STOP WASTING TIME ON?

WHAT FEAR HAS BEEN HOLDING YOU BACK FROM FULLY EMBRACING YOUR LIFE?

REFLECTION QUESTIONS: WHAT WOULD YOU DO WITH BORROWED TIME?

HOW WOULD YOU LIVE IF YOU TRULY BELIEVED THAT EVERY BREATH WAS A GIFT?
BECAUSE IT IS. AND SO ARE YOU.

WHERE IN YOUR LIFE HAVE YOU BEEN CONDITIONED TO STAY SMALL,
QUIET, OR AGREEABLE?

"

"You are not here
just to survive.

You are here to set
the world on fire
with your existence"

Lisa Lacy

CHAPTER

03

SAYING F'OFF TO TOXICITY BREAKING FREE FROM A NARCISSISTIC MARRIAGE

The Slow Erosion of Self

No one walks into a relationship expecting it to break them. When I met him, **I didn't see the red flags waving like warning signals in a storm.**

Love has a way of blinding you, convincing you that the good outweighs the bad, that the manipulation is just "concern," that the gaslighting is just "miscommunication," that the slow and steady **erosion of who you are** is somehow your fault.

By the time I realized the **extent of the damage,** I was already **drowning in it.**
A narcissistic relationship **isn't a thunderstorm;** it's a **slow, creeping flood.** It starts with small compromises, little allowances, and moments where you **second-guess your own intuition.**

- Did he really mean that?
- Maybe I overreacted.
- Maybe I'm just being sensitive.

And that's how it begins. The **constant questioning,** the **self-doubt,** the way your world starts **shrinking** around the ego of another person.

THE GASLIGHTING GAME

Gaslighting is one of the most insidious forms of **abuse** because it makes you **doubt your own reality**.

Conversations turned into battlegrounds where my own memories were twisted against me. He would rewrite history in real-time, turning my concerns into fabrications, my pain into "overreactions," my valid anger into "craziness."

- "That never happened."
- "You're imagining things."
- "You're too emotional."
- "You always want to argue."

It wasn't just that he lied, **it was that he made me believe I was the liar.**

I learned to **distrust my own emotions.** If I was upset, I told myself I was probably wrong. If I was hurt, I assumed I was being too sensitive. If **I felt unseen, unheard, discarded,** I convinced myself I was simply asking for too much. That's the thing about **narcissistic relationships,** they train you to apologize for needing basic human decency.

THE TURNING POINT

The day I finally said **F'OFF** wasn't quiet.
It wasn't calm.
It wasn't a peaceful goodbye.
It was **violent.**
It was **chaos.**
It was a **fight that left me battered, bruised, and barely breathing.**
I didn't just leave,
I fought my way out.
When **I finally stood up for myself,** when I **refused to be controlled,** the **rage** that had simmered beneath the surface of our marriage **exploded.**
He **lashed out.** I defended myself.

It escalated into a physical altercation so brutal that by the time it was over, **I was the one in handcuffs,** thrown into the back of a police car, charged, and left to process my escape from behind bars.

And the irony?

The injuries I sustained during that final fight triggered yet **another pulmonary embolism,** my body responding to **trauma** the only way it knew: **blood clots, suffocation, survival.**

This wasn't just a breakup.
This was a war.
A war I barely survived.

THE AFTERMATH
REBUILDING FROM NOTHING

People talk about **breakups** like they're just about **moving on.**
But leaving a **toxic relationship** isn't just about **walking away from another person;**
It's about **reclaiming yourself.**

Who was I without his voice in my head telling me I was unworthy, ungrateful, difficult, dramatic?

Who was I without the fear of **setting him off**, without the constant **emotional** exhaustion, without the **weight of his expectations crushing me?**

It took time.

For months, **I still flinched at the idea of expressing my own needs.** I hesitated before speaking up and felt the phantom guilt of "disappointing" someone who was no longer in my life.

But slowly, I started remembering who I was before him.

I started **laughing without waiting for permission.**
I started **trusting my gut instead of questioning it.**
I started saying **F'OFF** to anyone who tried to **make me feel small again.**

WHAT I LEARNED FROM ESCAPING A NARCISSIST

- 01 -

LOVE SHOULD NEVER FEEL LIKE WALKING ON EGGSHELLS.

If you're constantly afraid of upsetting someone;
That's not love, it's control.

- 02 -

GASLIGHTING IS ABUSE.

If someone makes you question your reality, your emotions,
or your experiences, they are manipulating you.

- 03 -

SILENCE IS AN ANSWER.

When someone dismisses your pain, invalidates your concerns,
or refuses to acknowledge your worth, believe them.
Stop explaining. Stop justifying. Just walk away.

- 04 -

YOU DON'T OWE ANYONE ENDLESS CHANCES.

Forgiveness is for you. Boundaries are for them.
Just because someone apologizes doesn't mean you have to stay.

- 05 -

SAYING F'OFF IS AN ACT OF SELF-LOVE.

Walking away from toxicity isn't being harsh, it's choosing peace over war,
clarity over confusion, freedom over control.

MASTERING THE F'OFF FRAMEWORK TO BREAK FREE FROM TOXICITY

F – FACE THE TRUTH

Toxicity thrives in denial. If you're constantly exhausted, constantly explaining yourself, or constantly doubting your own worth, face it. Name it. Own it.

Action Step: Write down the top three ways this relationship (or any toxic connection) has drained you. No excuses. No justifications. Just the truth.

MASTERING THE F'OFF FRAMEWORK TO BREAK FREE FROM TOXICITY

O – OWN YOUR BOUNDARIES

Emotional freedom starts when you stop giving toxic people access to your peace.
Action Step: Choose one boundary to reinforce today, whether it's blocking a number, saying no, or refusing to engage in manipulation tactics.

_____

_____

_____

_____

_____

_____

_____

_____

F – FULLY CHOOSE YOURSELF

Choosing yourself is not selfish. It's survival.
Action Step: Say this out loud:
"I will never apologize for demanding respect. I will never shrink myself to make someone else comfortable. I choose me."

F – FEARLESSLY TAKE ACTION

Freedom from toxicity requires action. It's not enough to know it's bad—you have to leave it behind.
Action Step: Take one immediate action to cut ties with toxicity today. Delete, block, walk away, stop engaging. Do it now.

SMALL RITUALS TO DETOX YOUR LIFE

- 01 -

THE "NO MORE EXCUSES" RULE

Each time you catch yourself justifying someone's toxic behavior, stop. Would you accept this from a stranger? If not, stop making excuses for them.

- 02 -

DAILY ENERGY AUDIT

At the end of each day, reflect: What gave me energy today? What drained me? If something consistently leaves you feeling empty, it's time to cut it out.

- 03 -

THE DOOR SLAM PRACTICE

The Door Slam Practice: Write a letter to the toxic person (you don't have to send it) saying everything you've held back. Then, rip it up or burn it.

THE "DOOR SLAM LETTER"

The Door Slam Practice – Write a letter to the toxic person (you don't have to send it) saying everything you've held back. Then, rip it up or burn it.

MINDSET SHIFTS TO BREAK FREE FROM MANIPULATION

- O1 -

LOVE SHOULD NEVER FEEL LIKE OBLIGATION OR FEAR.

- O2 -

IF YOU HAVE TO CONSTANTLY PROVE YOUR WORTH TO SOMEONE, THEY DON'T DESERVE YOU.

- O3 -

YOU DON'T NEED CLOSURE FROM TOXIC PEOPLE. LEAVING IS THE CLOSURE.

PRACTICAL STEPS TO RECLAIM YOUR EMOTIONAL FREEDOM

- 01 -

BLOCK & DELETE WITHOUT GUILT

You don't owe access to anyone who abuses your energy.

- 02 -

SET "NO CONTACT" BOUNDARIES

If possible, eliminate direct contact. If not, minimize interaction and remain emotionally detached.

- 03 -

REBUILD YOUR IDENTITY

Start exploring who you are outside of the toxic relationship.

REFLECTION QUESTIONS: DETOXING YOUR LIFE

WHO IN YOUR LIFE MAKES YOU FEEL SMALL, EXHAUSTED, OR UNWORTHY?

HAVE YOU EVER APOLOGIZED FOR ASKING FOR BASIC RESPECT? WHY?

REFLECTION QUESTIONS: DETOXING YOUR LIFE

WHEN WAS THE LAST TIME YOU IGNORED A RED FLAG?

_____

_____

_____

_____

_____

_____

_____

_____

_____

WHAT'S ONE THING YOU NEED TO WALK AWAY FROM, AND WHAT'S STOPPING YOU?

_____

_____

_____

_____

_____

_____

_____

_____

_____

"

BECAUSE THE MOMENT YOU DECIDE TO STOP TOLERATING TOXICITY IS THE MOMENT YOU START LIVING AGAIN.

WALKING AWAY FROM TOXICITY ISN'T WEAKNESS, IT'S THE BRAVEST THING YOU'LL EVER DO.

Lisa Lacy

CHAPTER
04

SAYING F'OFF TO LABELS
YOU ARE NOT YOUR DIAGNOSIS

The Weight of a Label

There's a moment in every mental health journey when you hear the words, the ones that are meant to **define you.**

- **Borderline Personality Disorder.**
- **Bipolar Disorder.**
- **C-PTSD.**

Words that land like a **sentence.** Like **a life you didn't sign up for.**
Some people say getting a diagnosis is **validating,** a moment of clarity that helps explain the **chaos inside.** For others, like me, it felt like being **shoved into a box** that I never belonged in. Like suddenly, I wasn't a **person** anymore, **I was a collection of symptoms.** A disorder. A **checklist. A statistic.** But here's the thing: **I am not my diagnosis.** And neither are you.

THE WORLD WANTS TO DEFINE YOU

The moment a **label** is attached to you, the world **changes** the way it looks at you.

- You stop being "complicated" and start being "unstable."
- Your emotions aren't just "big feelings" anymore; they're "mood swings."
- Your trauma responses aren't about what happened to you; they're a disorder that needs to be treated, managed, and controlled.

I've watched **people's expressions shift** when they hear the words **Borderline Personality Disorder**. I've seen the **assumptions** flicker across their faces.

- Oh, so you're crazy.
- Oh, so you're manipulative.
- Oh, so everything you say is invalid because your brain doesn't work like mine.

The **stigma** around mental illness isn't just about **misunderstanding**; it's about **power**. It's about **control**. It's about taking the most **painful, isolating experiences of your life** and turning them into a reason why you should be **dismissed.**

F'OFF to that.

LIVING WITH THE "DIAGNOSIS" STAMP

I spent **years** believing that my **disorders defined me.** That I was **doomed** to be unstable. That my **emotions were always wrong.**

- When I was **angry**, I asked myself, "Am I overreacting?" or "Is this just the BPD?"
- When I was **sad**, I told myself, "It's probably just the bipolar," not real sadness.
- When I was **triggered**, I whispered, "This is just the C-PTSD talking, not me."

Until one day, I realized **I was gaslighting myself.**
I had **internalized the voices** of everyone who had ever dismissed me. I had let a **diagnosis overshadow my reality**. And that was the moment I decided: **F'OFF.**

THE TRUTH ABOUT MENTAL HEALTH LABELS

YES, MENTAL HEALTH CONDITIONS ARE REAL.

YES, THEY AFFECT THE WAY WE PROCESS EMOTIONS, RELATIONSHIPS, AND THE WORLD AROUND US.

YES, HAVING A NAME FOR WHAT YOU'RE GOING THROUGH CAN SOMETIMES BE HELPFUL.

BUT HERE'S WHAT NO ONE TELLS YOU:

- 01 -

A DIAGNOSIS IS NOT A PERSONALITY.

Having **BPD** doesn't mean you're manipulative.
Having **bipolar disorder** doesn't mean you're unstable.
Having **C-PTSD** doesn't mean you're doomed to be stuck in trauma forever.

- 02 -

YOU ARE MORE THAN A LIST OF SYMPTOMS.

If you feel things deeply, that doesn't mean you're "too much."
If you react strongly, that doesn't mean you're "damaged."

- 03 -

THE MENTAL HEALTH SYSTEM LOVES A LABEL

But you don't have to accept it as your whole identity.
There is no 'one size fits all' for healing.

THE DAY I TOOK MY POWER BACK

I woke up one day and realized I had spent years **apologizing for who I was.** Years trying to prove that I was "**good enough**" despite my diagnoses.

And I was done.

- Done explaining my emotions like I was in a courtroom.
- Done tiptoeing around my own reactions.
- Done feeling like I had to "earn" love, respect, and basic human decency.

I stood up, looked in the mirror, and said it out loud: **F'OFF.**
To every doctor who had ever dismissed me. To every person who had ever used my diagnosis as an insult. To every self-doubt that whispered I was "too broken" to heal. **F'OFF. F'OFF. F'OFF. I decide who I am.** Not a label. Not a diagnosis. **Me.**

MASTERING THE F'OFF FRAMEWORK TO RECLAIM YOUR IDENTITY

F – FACE THE TRUTH

Your diagnosis does not define you. Your struggles do not make you less worthy. Face it. Name it. **Own your narrative.**

Action Step: Write down three things that make you who you are outside of any diagnosis. Your passions, your strengths, your essence.

1 - MY PASSION

2 - MY STRENGTHS

3 - MY ESSENCE

MASTERING THE F'OFF FRAMEWORK TO RECLAIM YOUR IDENTITY

O – OWN YOUR BOUNDARIES

You don't have to accept labels that don't serve you. You don't owe **explanations** for your emotions. You don't need to **prove** that your feelings are valid.
Action Step: The next time someone tries to **dismiss** your emotions because of a label, **call it out**: "No, I'm not 'just overreacting.' My feelings are real."
"My diagnosis doesn't make my words any less valid."

F – FULLY CHOOSE YOURSELF

You are not a disorder. You are a full human being.
Action Step: Say this out loud:
"I refuse to let a diagnosis define my worth. I am more than a label. I choose to live my life as my fullest, truest self."

F – FEARLESSLY TAKE ACTION

Healing is not about "fixing" yourself.
It's about embracing who you are, fully and unapologetically.
Action Step: Take one step today toward **living beyond your diagnosis.**
Whether it's engaging in a **hobby that makes you feel alive,** having a **conversation without apologizing for your emotions**, or refusing to let someone reduce you to a disorder.

SMALL RITUALS TO TAKE BACK YOUR IDENTITY

- 01 -

THE "WHO AM I?" LIST

Write down **10 things** that define you outside of your diagnosis.
Your **passions, strengths, quirks,** everything that makes you, you.

- 02 -

RECLAIM YOUR LANGUAGE

Stop introducing yourself with "I have [diagnosis]."
Instead, introduce yourself with **what lights you up.**

- 03 -

THE "NORMAL IS A LIE" AFFIRMATION

Every time you catch yourself thinking,
"**I wish I were normal.**" Remind yourself.
"**Normal is a myth. I am uniquely, beautifully me.**"

THE "WHO AM I" LIST

Write down 10 things that define you **outside of your diagnosis.**
Your passions, strengths, quirks, everything that makes you, you.

MINDSET SHIFTS TO ESCAPE THE BOX OF LABELS

- 01 -

A DIAGNOSIS IS A TOOL FOR UNDERSTANDING,

not a definition of who you are.

- 02 -

YOU ARE NOT A DISORDER.

You are a full human being.

- 03 -

HEALING IS NOT ABOUT "FIXING" YOURSELF

it's about learning to live authentically.

PRACTICAL STEPS TO TAKE BACK CONTROL

- 01 -

REFUSE TO BE DEFINED BY OTHERS

The next time someone uses your diagnosis against you "Oh, that's just your anxiety talking." **Call them out:** "No, that's just me setting a boundary."

- 02 -

PRIORITIZE HOLISTIC HEALING

Therapy is helpful, but so are other things: **movement, creativity, and connection.** Explore beyond what the system prescribes.

- 03 -

CURATE A SUPPORT SYSTEM

Surround yourself with people who **see you**, **not just your diagnosis.** If your current circle keeps reinforcing the label, **find new people who uplift you.**

REFLECTION QUESTIONS: DEFINING YOURSELF BEYOND LABELS

WHAT IS ONE THING ABOUT YOU THAT HAS NOTHING TO DO WITH YOUR DIAGNOSIS?

HAVE YOU EVER LET A LABEL DEFINE WHAT YOU THINK YOU'RE CAPABLE OF?

REFLECTION QUESTIONS: DEFINING YOURSELF BEYOND LABELS

IF YOU STRIPPED AWAY EVERY DIAGNOSIS, EVERY EXPECTATION, EVERY BOX PEOPLE HAVE PUT YOU IN, WHO ARE YOU AT YOUR CORE?

WHAT IS ONE WAY YOU CAN START RECLAIMING YOUR IDENTITY TODAY?

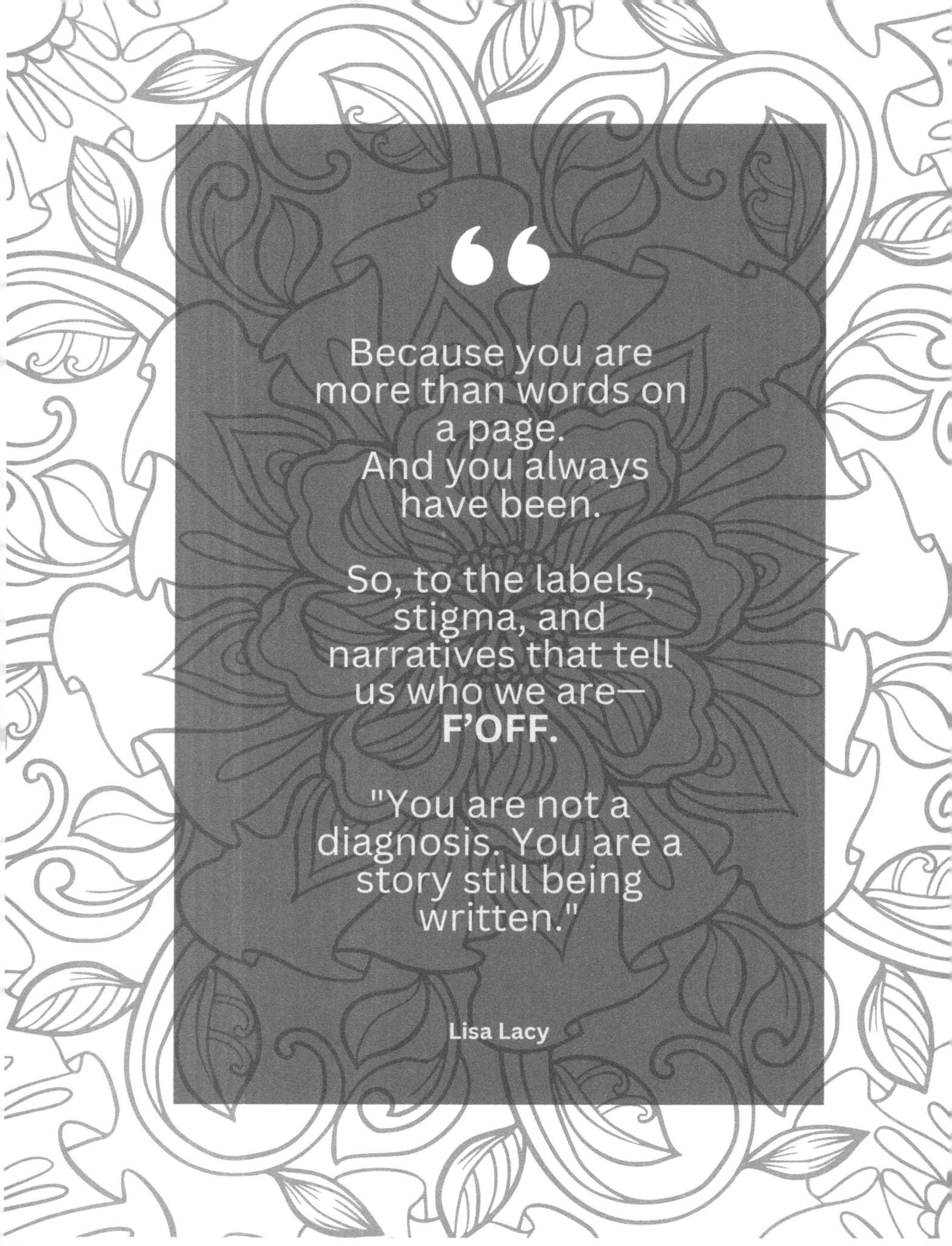

"

Because you are more than words on a page.
And you always have been.

So, to the labels, stigma, and narratives that tell us who we are—
F'OFF.

"You are not a diagnosis. You are a story still being written."

Lisa Lacy

CHAPTER

05

SAYING F'OFF TO ADDICTION RECLAIMING MY MIND, BODY & POWER

The Chains We Choose

Addiction doesn't begin with destruction. **It begins with comfort.**
It starts as a whisper, not a scream. A subtle promise:

- This will help.
- This will make it easier.
- This will quiet the chaos inside.

For me, addiction wasn't about getting high. It wasn't about **partying, rebellion, or even fun.**

IT WAS SURVIVAL
A WAY TO SILENCE EMOTIONS

I didn't understand. A way to escape the **weight of everything** I never learned how to process. I was **never taught** how to sit with my pain. No one showed me how to move through **grief, anger, loneliness, or disappointment** in a way that didn't destroy me. So, like many of us, I was conditioned to **suppress, ignore, and numb.**

At first, it was small.
- A drink to take the edge off.
- A pill to smooth out the rough patches of reality.
- Just **something** to help me cope.

But addiction is never satisfied with "just a little."
What once seemed like a choice turned into a **compulsion, a habit, dependency.**
Before I even realized what had happened, it had wrapped its chains around me so **tightly** that I didn't know where it ended and I began.

For **20 years**, I lived in a cycle of self-medication.
20 years of chasing numbness instead of healing.
20 years of believing the lie that I needed something outside of myself to survive my emotions.
20 years of not knowing who I was without the substances that had become part of my identity. And the scariest part? **... I thought I had control.**

THE ILLUSION OF CONTROL

People think addiction is obvious.
They picture **rock bottom moments,** overdoses, arrests, homelessness, interventions. They assume it looks like **chaos, destruction, and ruin.** But addiction wears **many disguises.**

Sometimes, it appears that the person seems **completely functional,** still **showing up to work or laughing at the right moments.** The one who convinces themselves that they **don't have a problem** because they **aren't at rock-bottom yet.** That was me.
I told myself: "I don't have a problem, I'm fine. I still get things done, I still show up."

But addiction isn't just about how much you use; It's about why you use, and what happens when you try to stop.

And when I tried to stop? The truth hit me like a wrecking ball; **I didn't know how to exist without it.** Without the substances, my emotions **came back in full force.**
- The **anxiety.**
- The **anger.**
- The **grief.**
- The **rawness of everything I had been running from for decades.**

And it **terrified me.**

WHY WE STAY STUCK

There's a reason people stay trapped in addiction for years, sometimes forever.

It's not because they're **weak.**
It's not because they **want to destroy themselves.**
It's because addiction feels **safer than healing.**
Facing your pain head-on? That's terrifying.
Sitting with emotions you've spent a lifetime avoiding? That feels like **torture.**
Sobriety isn't just about quitting the substance; it's about learning to live **without the crutch** you've always had to lean on.

- For years, I convinced myself that **I needed it.**
- I can't function without this.
- I'll always struggle with my emotions, so I might as well manage them this way.
- I've been doing this for too long. It's part of who I am.

But those were just lies that I told myself because I was too scared to face the truth:
I wasn't broken.
I was just **untrained** in emotional intelligence.
And that was something I could change.

THE MOMENT I SAID F'OFF TO ADDICTION

There wasn't just one moment. There were many.
- **Rock-bottom moments,** looking in the mirror and not recognizing myself.
- **Near-miss moments,** and the realization that I was playing Russian roulette with my health, my relationships, my future.

And then, there was the moment I decided:
I was done.
Not because I had to.
Not because someone forced me to.
But because I finally understood that **I deserved better.**
And so, I said it.
F'OFF.
To the voice that told me I needed it.
To the lie that said I wasn't strong enough.
To the fear that tried to keep me in chains.
I chose myself.
And I never looked back.

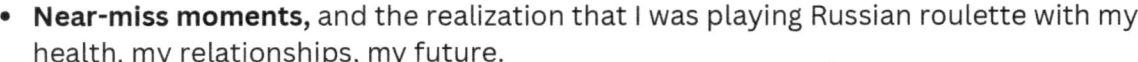

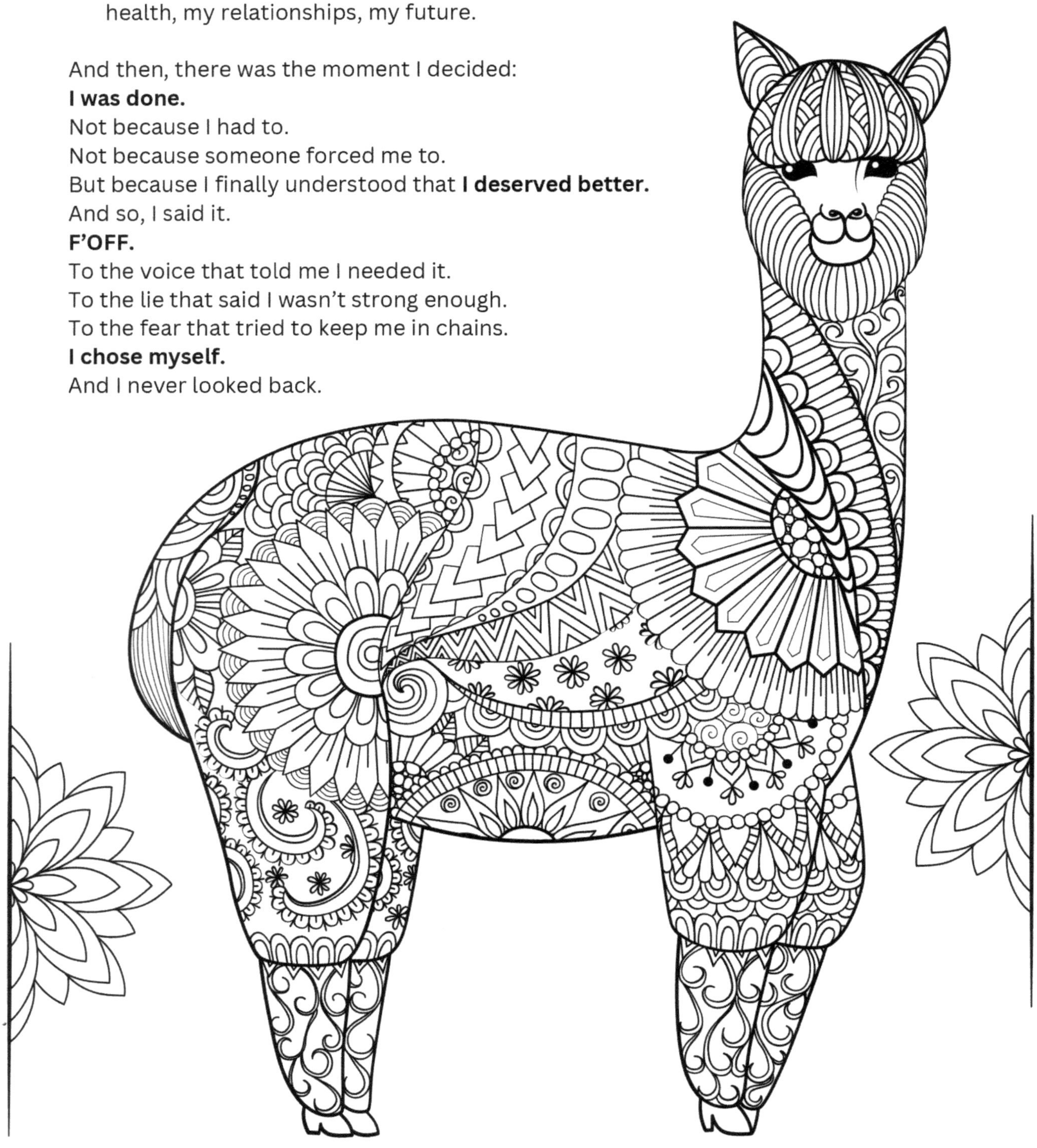

MASTERING THE F'OFF FRAMEWORK TO BREAK FREE FROM ADDICTION

F – FACE THE TRUTH

Denial keeps you stuck. Addiction doesn't start with the substance; it starts with avoiding emotions. Face it. Name it. Own your truth.

Action Step: Write down what you've been running from. What emotion, memory, or fear have you been numbing? No shame. No judgment. Just honesty.

MASTERING THE F'OFF FRAMEWORK TO RECLAIM YOUR IDENTITY

O – OWN YOUR BOUNDARIES

You don't owe addiction another second of your time.
Action Step: Set a clear boundary with yourself:
"I will no longer use [substance] to avoid my emotions."
"I choose to deal with my feelings in a way that serves me."

F – FULLY CHOOSE YOURSELF

Choosing sobriety is choosing yourself.
It's reclaiming your mind, body, and power.
Action Step: Say this out loud:
"I don't need a substance to survive my emotions.
I choose clarity. I choose freedom. I choose me."

F – FEARLESSLY TAKE ACTION

Addiction won't leave quietly. You have to take action.
Action Step: Take one immediate action to remove the temptation, throw it away, and cancel plans with toxic people. Tell someone you trust to hold you accountable. Do it now.

PLEDGE:

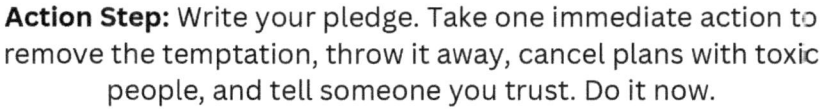

Action Step: Write your pledge. Take one immediate action to remove the temptation, throw it away, cancel plans with toxic people, and tell someone you trust. Do it now.

SMALL RITUALS TO BREAK THE CYCLE

- 01 -

THE "SIT WITH IT" PRACTICE

Every time I felt the urge to escape,
I sat with the discomfort for 10 minutes.
No distractions. No numbing. Just breathing and feeling.

- 02 -

THE DAILY CHECK-IN

Every morning, I asked myself: **How do I feel today?**
Instead of running, **I honored the answer.**

- 03 -

REPLACING THE RITUAL

Addiction thrives on routine. So, I created new ones: tea instead of
alcohol, journaling instead of numbing.

MY NEW ROUTINE:

Action Step: Take one immediate action to remove the temptation. Addiction thrives on routine, so today you need to establish a new one. Describe a hobby or interest that will sustain you.

MINDSET SHIFTS TO REWIRE MY BRAIN

- 01 -

I DON'T NEED TO ESCAPE MY EMOTIONS.

I need to learn from them.

- 02 -

ADDICTION WASN'T MY WEAKNESS.

It was my survival mechanism that no longer serves me.

- 03 -

HEALING ISN'T ABOUT PERFECTION.

It's about making one better decision at a time.

- 04 -

I DON'T "OWE" MY OLD SELF ANYTHING.

I am allowed to evolve, grow, and break free.

PRACTICAL STEPS TO STAY FREE

- 01 -

REMOVE THE TRIGGERS

Clean out your space, cut ties with people who enable you, and avoid places that pull you back in.

- 02 -

BUILD A SUPPORT SYSTEM

Surround yourself with people who hold you accountable and **celebrate your growth.**

- 03 -

EMBRACE THE CRAVINGS INSTEAD OF FIGHTING THEM

Say: **"This feeling is temporary. I don't have to act on it."**

REFLECTION QUESTIONS: DEFINING YOURSELF BEYOND LABELS

WHAT HAVE YOU BEEN USING TO NUMB EMOTIONS INSTEAD OF PROCESSING THEM?

WHAT FEELINGS SCARE YOU THE MOST? WHY?

REFLECTION QUESTIONS: DEFINING YOURSELF BEYOND LABELS

WHAT IS ONE THING YOU CAN USE TO REPLACE YOUR UNHEALTHY COPING MECHANISM?

WHO IN YOUR LIFE SUPPORTS YOUR HEALING, AND WHO KEEPS YOU STUCK?

66

TRUE FREEDOM ISN'T JUST BREAKING THE
ADDICTION,
IT'S RECLAIMING YOURSELF.

ADDICTION IS A LIE THAT SAYS YOU NEED A
SUBSTANCE TO SURVIVE. THE TRUTH IS, YOU ARE
STRONGER THAN YOU EVER KNEW.

Lisa Lacy

CHAPTER

06

SAYING F'OFF TO ABANDONMENT BREAKING FREE FROM MY FATHER'S SHADOW

The Ghost in My Blood

Some fathers leave quietly, like smoke fading into the sky; they disappear without a trace. A memory that lingers but never fully forms. Mine didn't. My father wasn't just **gone;** he was a **storm** that ripped through my life, leaving **wreckage in his wake. A biker. A convicted felon. A man hardened by a life I never got to fully understand. Ten years behind bars.** But in truth, he had been absent **long before that.** And yet, despite his **absence,** he cast a **shadow** over my **entire existence.** It didn't matter that he wasn't there. **His ghost still haunted me.**

I SPENT YEARS TRYING TO FILL THE SPACE HE LEFT BEHIND.

- Searching for **approval**
- **Chasing validation**
- **Clinging** to love like it was the **only thing keeping me from falling apart.**

Because when your own **father walks away**, it plants a question **deep inside of you:**

What was so wrong with me that he didn't stay?
No one says it out loud, but it **becomes part of you.**
It seeps into your **relationships, your choices, your identity.**
You learn to **crave validation like it's oxygen.**
You tell yourself you're **strong, independent, unbothered.**
But deep down, **the wound still bleeds.**
Until one day, I realized something: **My father didn't define me.**
His absence wasn't a **reflection of my worth; it was a reflection of his own demons.**
And I was done letting his **choices** dictate my **life.**
It was time to say **F'OFF** to **abandonment.**

THE ABANDONMENT SCAR

People think abandonment is just about **physical absence.**
That if someone leaves, it **only** affects the relationship itself.
But **abandonment rewires your brain.** It changes the way you see **yourself, the way you trust, the way you engage with the world.**

FOR ME, IT SHOWED UP IN WAYS I DIDN'T EVEN RECOGNIZE AT FIRST:

- 01 -

THE FEAR OF REJECTION

I bent over backward for people who didn't deserve me because **I was terrified of being left again.**

- 02 -

THE CONSTANT NEED FOR APPROVAL

If someone validated me, I clung to it like a **lifeline.**
If they didn't, I spiraled.

- 03 -

THE UNSHAKABLE RAGE

I didn't just feel hurt. I felt **angry,** furious that someone could leave me behind **like I was nothing.**

- 04 -

THE SELF-DOUBT

No matter how much I accomplished, a voice inside whispered, **You'll never be enough.**

ABANDONMENT DOESN'T JUST HURT, IT REPROGRAMS YOU.

But here's the truth:

You are not what someone else did to you.
I wasn't the **daughter my father left behind.**
I wasn't the **kid waiting for a man who never showed up.**
I wasn't the **empty seat at the dinner table, the unanswered phone call, or the forgotten memory.** I was me. And I was **done carrying his absence like a weight around my neck.**

THE MOMENT I STOPPED WAITING

There wasn't some **dramatic movie moment** where I had an epiphany and **instantly healed.** It was **years of unraveling.**
- Years of **unlearning** the belief that I was **unworthy of love.**
- Years of **rewriting the story** that said I was **broken.**

But there was **a moment, one that changed everything.**
A regular day. **Nothing special.** I was sitting alone, caught in **one of those spirals** where my mind replayed **every moment** I had ever felt abandoned.

And then, a thought hit me like a wrecking ball:
I've been waiting for a father who was never coming back.
Waiting for an **apology, closure, or some explanation that will help me make sense of it all.** And for what? He wasn't **losing sleep over this.** He wasn't **trapped in the cycle.**
I was. I had been carrying his absence like it was **my burden to bear.**

AND IN THAT MOMENT, I MADE A DECISION:

I am done waiting.
I am done hurting.
I am done letting a ghost run my life.

That was the day **I stopped looking for something that was never going to come.**
That was the day **I chose myself.**

MASTERING THE F'OFF FRAMEWORK TO HEAL ABANDONMENT

F – FACE THE TRUTH

Abandonment leaves wounds, but it does not define your worth.
Face it. Name it. Own your truth.
Action Step: Write down **one belief** you've carried because of abandonment.
Challenge it. Instead of "I wasn't enough," say:
"They weren't capable of showing up for me."

MASTERING THE F'OFF FRAMEWORK TO RECLAIM YOUR IDENTITY

O – OWN YOUR BOUNDARIES

You don't have to prove your worth to anyone.
Action Step: The next time you feel yourself **over-explaining, over-giving, or chasing approval,** pause. **Ask yourself: Am I doing this because I want to, or because I fear being left behind?**

_____

_____

_____

_____

_____

_____

_____

_____

_____

F – FULLY CHOOSE YOURSELF

You are not missing a piece—you are already whole.
Action Step: Say this out loud: **"I am not defined by who left me. I am defined by who I choose to become."**

F – FEARLESSLY TAKE ACTION

Healing starts when you decide to stop waiting.
Action Step: Take **one immediate step** toward closure, **write the letter you'll never send, say the words you've held in, let go of the need for an apology.**

THE "LETTER"

Action Step: Take one immediate step toward closure, write the letter you'll never send, say the words you've held in, let go of the need for an apology.

SMALL RITUALS TO HEAL ABANDONMENT WOUNDS

- 01 -

THE "I AM HERE" RITUAL

Every morning, **place your hand on your chest** and remind yourself:
"I am here. I am whole. I am enough."

- 02 -

REWRITING THE STORY

Write a letter to the person who abandoned you, **not to send, but to release it from your body.** Burn it, rip it up, let it go.

- 03 -

THE "WHO SHOWED UP?" PRACTICE

Instead of fixating on the ones **who left,** list the people **who stayed.**

THE APOLOGY LETTER

Write a letter to the person who abandoned you, not to send, but to release it from your body. Burn it, rip it up, let it go.

MINDSET SHIFTS TO BREAK FREE

- 01 -

MY FATHER'S ABSENCE WAS HIS DECISION.

It was never about me.

- 02 -

I DON'T HAVE TO PROVE MY WORTH TO ANYONE.

I was always enough.

- 03 -

I AM NOT MISSING A PIECE.

I am already whole.

- 04 -

LOVE IS NOT SOMETHING I HAVE TO CHASE.

The right people will never make me beg for it.

PRACTICAL STEPS TO STOP SEEKING EXTERNAL VALIDATION

- 01 -

DETACH FROM THE NARRATIVE

Instead of "My father didn't love me," try "My father wasn't capable of loving me in the way I needed, but that does not define my worth."

- 02 -

CUT THE CORD WITH "PROVING" YOURSELF

Stop over-explaining, over-giving, and over-apologizing just to keep people around.

- 03 -

RECOGNIZE HEALTHY VS. UNHEALTHY ATTACHMENT

If someone's absence **destroys you**, ask yourself:
"Am I reacting to them or to the ghost of my father leaving?"

- 04 -

CREATE YOUR OWN CLOSURE

If you're waiting for **an apology,** stop. If you're waiting for them to **acknowledge your pain,** let go. Closure isn't something you **get,** it's something you **give yourself.**

REFLECTION QUESTIONS: RECLAIMING YOUR POWER

WHO IN YOUR PAST MADE YOU FEEL ABANDONED, AND HOW HAS THAT SHAPED YOUR RELATIONSHIPS TODAY?

_____

WHAT FALSE BELIEF ABOUT YOURSELF CAME FROM THAT ABANDONMENT? (EXAMPLE: "I'M NOT WORTHY OF LOVE.")

_____

REFLECTION QUESTIONS: RECLAIMING YOUR POWER

HOW CAN YOU START SHOWING UP FOR YOURSELF INSTEAD OF WAITING FOR SOMEONE ELSE TO?

WHAT DOES UNCONDITIONAL LOVE LOOK LIKE TO YOU? AND ARE YOU GIVING IT TO YOURSELF?

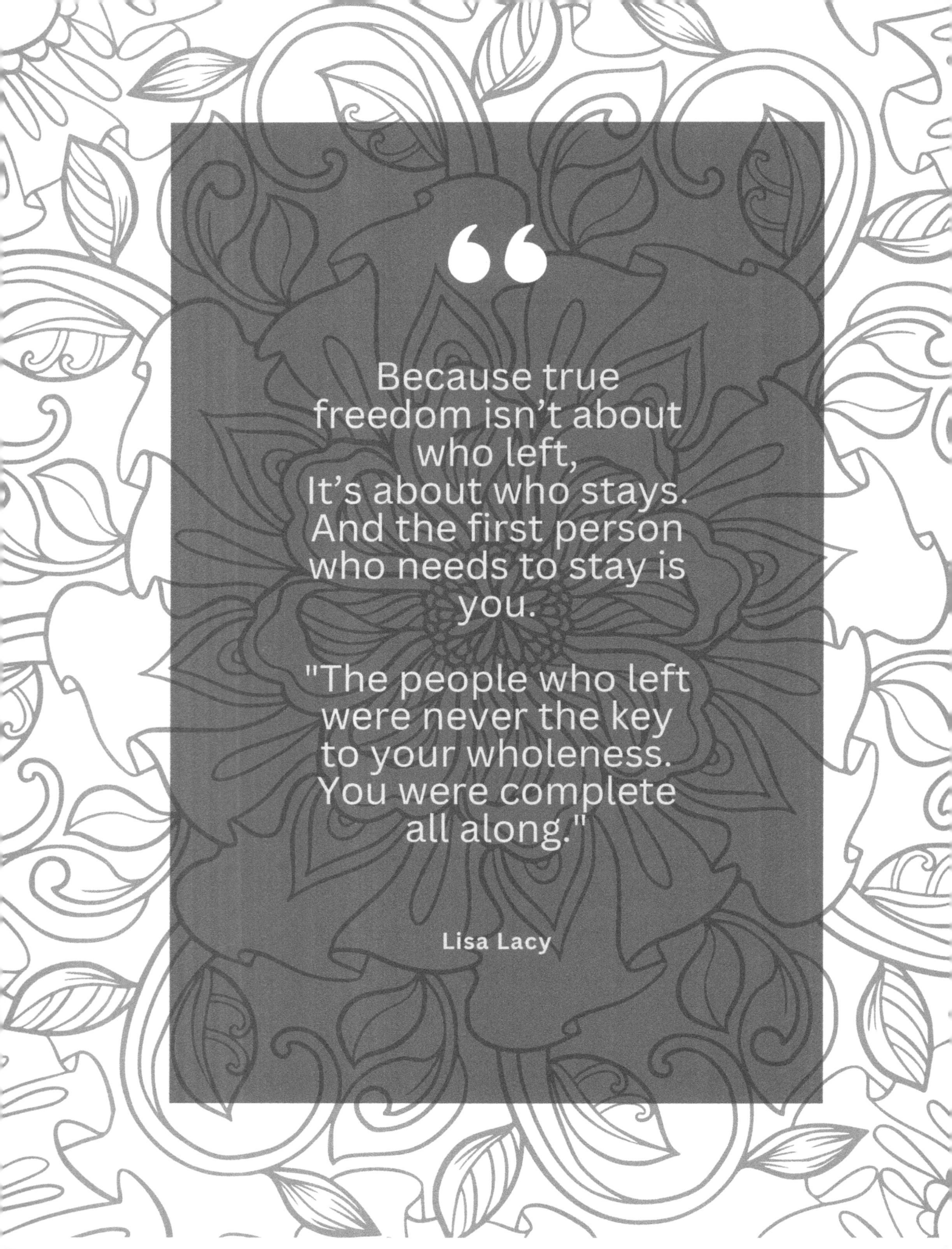

"

Because true
freedom isn't about
who left,
It's about who stays.
And the first person
who needs to stay is
you.

"The people who left
were never the key
to your wholeness.
You were complete
all along."

Lisa Lacy

CHAPTER

07

SAYING F'OFF TO FAWNING BREAKING FREE FROM 50 YEARS OF PEOPLE-PLEASING

The Prison of Pleasing

Fifty years. That's how long I spent putting **everyone else before myself.**

- **Fifty years** of smoothing things over, keeping the peace, and making myself small so that others could be comfortable.
- **Fifty years** of bending until I almost broke, of swallowing my truth because I was terrified of conflict, rejection, or disappointing someone.
- **Fifty years** of becoming whoever people needed me to be while losing sight of **who I actually was.**

It wasn't just a **bad habit, it was a trauma response;** one I didn't even know had a name. **It's calle**d fawning, **the fourth trauma** response, alongside **fight, flight, and freeze.** But instead of **running, fighting, or shutting down,** I learned to **survive by being a people pleaser.** It's the **deep, unconscious urge** to keep people happy so they **won't leave.** The automatic reflex to **put others' needs above your own,** not because you **want to,** but because somewhere along the way, your **nervous system learned:** **If I make everyone happy, I'll be safe;** and for five decades, **that's precisely what I did.**

HOW THE FAWN RESPONSE CONTROLLED MY LIFE

People think of people-pleasers as just being "nice."
But **fawning isn't about kindness, it's about fear.**

- **I said yes when I meant no;** because saying no felt like **rejection,** and rejection felt like **danger.**
- **I apologized for things that weren't my fault,** because keeping the **peace** was more important than standing my **ground.**
- **I avoided confrontation at all costs** because conflict triggered the deep, buried fear that I would **lose the people I love, their respect, or my sense of security.**
- **I anticipated people's needs before they even voiced them,** because if I could meet their expectations before they had to ask, **maybe they would stay.**
- **I lost myself in relationships,** because if I could be exactly what someone wanted, **maybe they wouldn't leave.**

It didn't matter whether it was **family, friends, partners, or bosses, I molded myself** to fit **whatever version of me they wanted.**

THE RESULT?

- 01 -

I WAS EXHAUSTED - BURNT OUT - RESENTFUL.

- 02 -

I WAS ALWAYS GIVING BUT NEVER RECEIVING.

- 03 -

I DIDN'T EVEN KNOW WHO I WAS WITHOUT OTHER PEOPLE'S EXPECTATIONS.

WHERE THE FAWN RESPONSE BEGINS

Fawning isn't something you choose; it's something you're conditioned to do.

For me, it started **young.**
I grew up in an environment where **peacekeeping was a matter of survival.**
Maybe it was a **volatile household.**
Maybe it was an **unpredictable parent.**
Maybe it was the **fear of abandonment.**
Whatever it was, my nervous system learned:

- Conflict = danger
- Disapproval = rejection
- Rejection = being alone
- Being alone = not safe

And so, **I adapted.**
I learned to **read the room like a mind-reader.**

- I could **sense tension before it erupted.**
- I could **shift my tone, words, and entire personality** just to keep things **"okay."**
- I became the fixer, **the caretaker, the chameleon,** whatever role was needed to maintain **harmony.**

At first, it seemed like a **strength.**

- People **liked me.**
- They saw me as **reliable, easygoing, "so nice."**

But underneath... **I was screaming.**
Because here's the thing they don't tell you about people-pleasing:
It isn't love. It's self-betrayal.

THE BREAKING POINT

For fifty years, I played the role.

I said the **right things,** kept my **emotions in check,** and made sure **everyone else was happy.** But one day, **something inside me snapped.**
I was in a conversation, one of those moments where **someone expected too much,** where I felt the **familiar weight of obligation pressing down on me.**
And instead of smiling, nodding, and agreeing **like I always did…** I heard it.
That small, fiery, forbidden voice inside me that had been **buried for five decades.**
"No." Just one word. **Small but earth-shattering.**
I saw their face change, **confusion, maybe frustration.**
The **old me** would have **panicked** at that reaction, rushing to **explain, justify, and backpedal,** but this time? **I didn't.**
I let the **silence stretch** and the **discomfort settle.** I released myself from the responsibility of fixing everything. And you know what? **The world didn't end.**
And that was the moment I realized: **I was free.**

MASTERING THE F'OFF FRAMEWORK TO STOP PEOPLE-PLEASING

F – FACE THE TRUTH

Pleasing everyone is not love, it's fear. And it's time to unlearn it.
Face it. Name it. **Own your truth.**
Action Step: Write down **three times** you said yes **when you meant no.**
What were you afraid would happen if you had said no?

MASTERING THE F'OFF FRAMEWORK TO RECLAIM YOUR IDENTITY

O – OWN YOUR BOUNDARIES

You are not responsible for managing everyone else's emotions.
Action Step: The next time you feel the **urge to over-explain a boundary,** stop.
Let it stand on its own. Example: Instead of "I'm sorry, I just can't," say:
"No, that doesn't work for me." "I'm not available for that."

_____

_____

_____

_____

_____

_____

_____

F – FULLY CHOOSE YOURSELF

You are allowed to take up space. You are allowed to disappoint people.
Action Step: Say this out loud: **"My needs are just as important as anyone else's. I do not exist to make everyone else comfortable."**

F – FEARLESSLY TAKE ACTION

People-pleasing doesn't fade on its own—you have to challenge it.
Action Step: Say no to something **this week** that you normally would have said yes to **just to keep the peace.**

SMALL RITUALS TO BREAK THE PEOPLE-PLEASING CYCLE

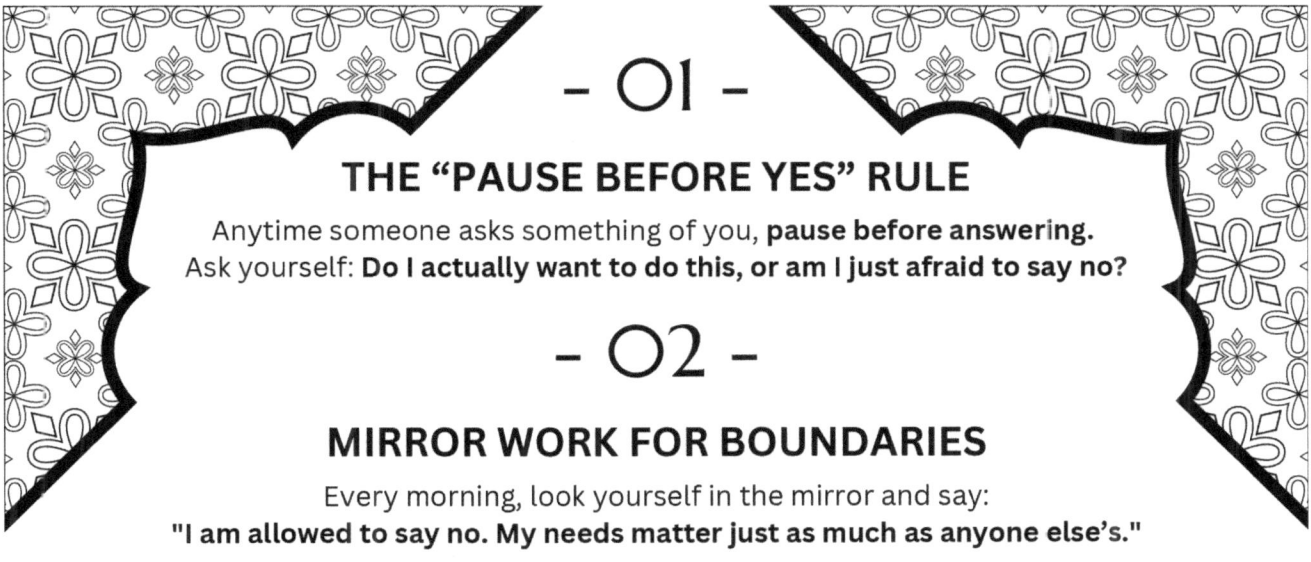

- 01 -

THE "PAUSE BEFORE YES" RULE

Anytime someone asks something of you, **pause before answering.**
Ask yourself: **Do I actually want to do this, or am I just afraid to say no?**

- 02 -

MIRROR WORK FOR BOUNDARIES

Every morning, look yourself in the mirror and say:
"I am allowed to say no. My needs matter just as much as anyone else's."

- 03 -

THE "SIT WITH THE DISCOMFORT" CHALLENGE

The next time you say no, resist the urge to explain.
Let the silence be awkward. Let the other person react.
You are not responsible for fixing their feelings.

MINDSET SHIFTS TO UNLEARN FAWNING

- 01 -

SAYING NO IS NOT SELFISH. IT'S SELF-RESPECT.

- 02 -

IF SOMEONE ONLY VALUES ME WHEN I'M COMPLIANT, THEY DON'T TRULY CARE ABOUT ME.

- 03 -

DISCOMFORT IS NOT DANGER. CONFLICT IS NOT CATASTROPHE.

- 04 -

I AM NOT RESPONSIBLE FOR MANAGING EVERYONE ELSE'S EMOTIONS.

PRACTICAL STEPS TO RECLAIM YOUR POWER

- 01 -

START SMALL

Practice saying **"no"** in low-stakes situations.

- 02 -

DETACH FROM PEOPLE'S REACTIONS

Their **disappointment** is not your **problem** to fix.

- 03 -

WRITE A "PERMISSION SLIP" TO YOURSELF

"I give myself permission to disappoint people
if it means protecting my peace."

- 04 -

RE-EVALUATE YOUR RELATIONSHIPS

Who respects your boundaries, and who
only values you when you comply?

REFLECTION QUESTIONS: RECLAIMING YOUR VOICE

WHEN WAS THE LAST TIME YOU IGNORED YOUR OWN NEEDS TO PLEASE SOMEONE ELSE?

WHAT'S THE WORST THING YOU IMAGINE HAPPENING IF YOU SAY "NO"?
IS IT REALLY THAT BAD?

REFLECTION QUESTIONS: RECLAIMING YOUR VOICE

WHO IN YOUR LIFE MAKES YOU FEEL GUILTY FOR HAVING BOUNDARIES?

HOW WOULD YOUR LIFE CHANGE IF YOU STOPPED TRYING TO KEEP EVERYONE HAPPY?

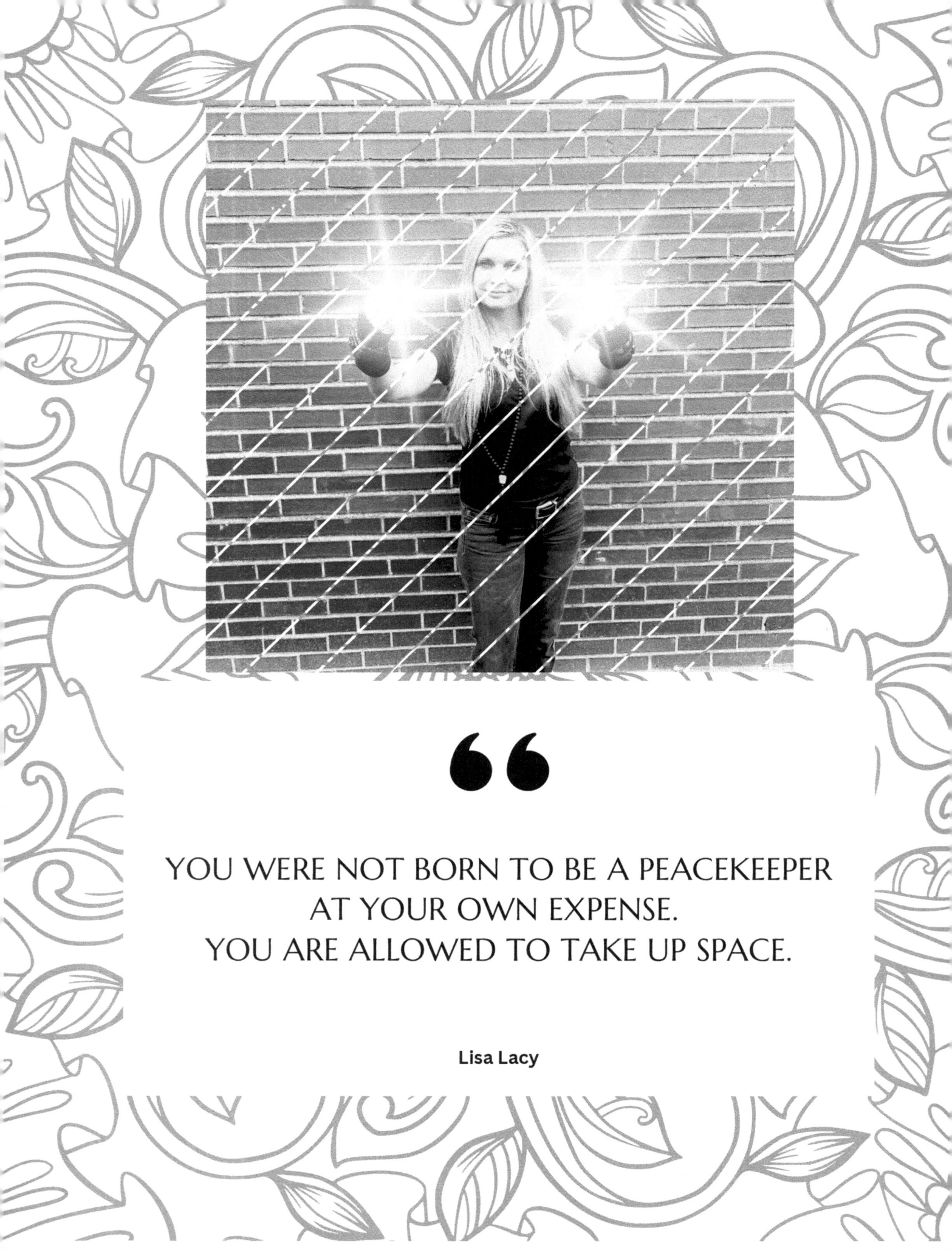

> **❝**
>
> YOU WERE NOT BORN TO BE A PEACEKEEPER
> AT YOUR OWN EXPENSE.
> YOU ARE ALLOWED TO TAKE UP SPACE.
>
> **Lisa Lacy**

CHAPTER

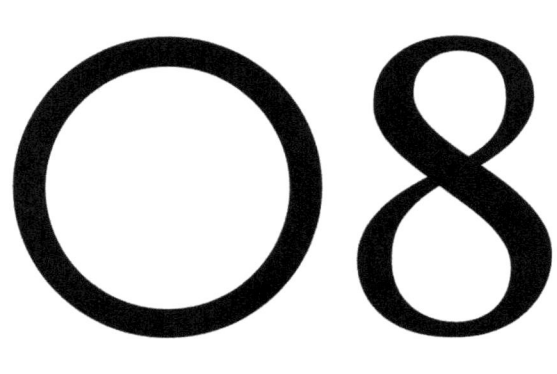

SAYING F'OFF TO GENERATIONAL TRAUMA & BECOMING THE CYCLE BREAKER

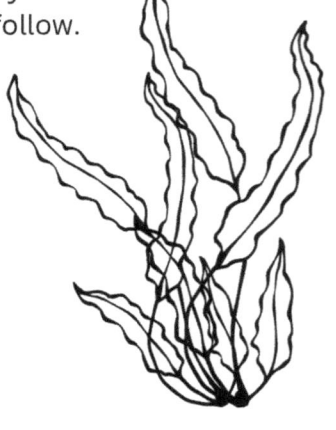

The Blood We Inherit

Some legacies come wrapped in **gold.** Others come wrapped in **grief, violence, and wounds so deep** they leave scars on the souls of those who never even lived through them. I was **born into a legacy of pain.**

My mother was only **twelve years old** when she watched her own mother **get beaten to death by her stepfather.** Murdered by the man who was **supposed to love and protect her.**
And then, at just **fifteen years old,** my mother had me. She was **a child raising a child.** A girl **haunted** by the trauma of her past, **now tasked with shaping the future of someone else.**
I didn't just inherit her **DNA.** I inherited her **fears, her pain, her survival instincts.** I carry the echoes of what she had been through.

Because that's what trauma does.
It's a legacy that refuses to die and gets **passed down,** like an **heirloom** nobody wants.
It lives in the nervous system and is carried in the DNA of the generations to follow.

- It teaches daughters to **flinch at raised voices.**
- It teaches sons to **mistake control for love.**
- It teaches entire bloodlines that pain is just part of the family tradition.

And if no one **stops it?**
It keeps going.
Until someone stands up and says,
"F'OFF. This cycle ends with me."

THE SCIENCE OF INHERITED TRAUMA (EPIGENETICS AND THE GHOSTS IN OUR DNA)

People love to say, "The past is in the past."

However, the past is **alive within us,** tightly woven into the way our **bodies respond to stress,** how we **handle relationships,** and our **perception of the world.**
Science calls it **epigenetics** —the idea that **trauma isn't just emotional; it alters our genes,** changing the way our bodies and minds **react to danger, even in subsequent generations.**

Studies show that:

- **Children of Holocaust survivors** have different stress responses than those whose parents didn't experience genocide.
- **Descendants of enslaved people** often show **higher cortisol levels (the stress hormone)** even in safe environments.
- **People from war-torn countries** carry **trauma responses** they never personally experienced.

Because **trauma doesn't start with you.**
But if you're willing to fight for it?
It can end with you.

THE MOMENT I DECIDED TO BE THE CYCLE BREAKER

For most of my life, I carried my trauma like a **second skin.**
I absorbed my **mother's pain** without even realizing it.
I didn't just inherit her story; **I inherited her fear of abandonment, her inability to trust, and her deep-rooted belief that love and pain were intertwined.**
I made all the **same mistakes. put my trust in the wrong people,** accepted **too little,** gave way **too much. I allowed** myself to be **disrespected, hurt, and used,** all because, deep down, my nervous system had learned that **this was what love felt like.**
And then one day, I looked at myself and thought:
"How much longer am I going to let dead people dictate my life?"
My grandmother's story **ended in violence;** my mother's story was **shaped by survival.**
But **my story...** That was still being written. And I refused to let it be **another chapter in the same damn tragedy.**

BECOMING THE CYCLE BREAKER (WITHOUT LOSING YOURSELF IN THE PROCESS)

Being a cycle breaker isn't just about **recognizing the trauma;** it's about **refusing to pass it on.** But that doesn't mean it's easy.

Because breaking cycles means:

- 01 -

HEALING WOUNDS YOU DIDN'T CREATE.

- 02 -

RELEARNING EVERYTHING YOU THOUGHT WAS NORMAL.

- 03 -

BECOMING THE PARENT YOU NEVER HAD.

- 04 -

CHOOSING GROWTH OVER COMFORT, EVEN WHEN IT HURTS.

And sometimes?

It means **walking away from the people who want to keep you stuck in the cycle.**
Because when you heal, **you become a mirror to those who haven't.**
And not everyone **wants to face their reflection.**

MASTERING THE F'OFF FRAMEWORK TO BREAK GENERATIONAL TRAUMA

F – FACE THE TRUTH

Cycles don't break themselves. If you don't face the pattern, you will repeat it.
Face it. Name it. Own your truth.
Action Step: Write down one **generational pattern** you refuse to pass down.
Say it out loud: "It ends with me."

MASTERING THE F'OFF FRAMEWORK TO BREAK GENERATIONAL TRAUMA

O – OWN YOUR BOUNDARIES

Healing means disrupting the cycle. And not everyone will like that.
Action Step: Set a **clear boundary** with family members who try to keep you stuck.
Example: "I will not tolerate toxic conversations."
"I will not be guilt-tripped into old patterns."

_____

_____

_____

_____

_____

_____

_____

_____

F – FULLY CHOOSE YOURSELF

You are not responsible for carrying their pain,
only for healing your own.
Action Step: Say this out loud:**"I do not have to live the life of my ancestors. I choose differently."**

F – FEARLESSLY TAKE ACTION

Breaking cycles requires action, not just awareness.
Action Step: Take one concrete step today, whether it's seeking therapy, cutting off toxic relationships, or unlearning old beliefs.

SMALL RITUALS TO BREAK GENERATIONAL TRAUMA

- 01 -

THE "REPARENTING" PRACTICE

Every time you **criticize yourself,** ask:
"Would I say this to a child who just wanted love?"
Rewrite the thought with **kindness.**

- 02 -

BREAKING THE PATTERN IN REAL TIME

When you **react out of fear, insecurity, or unhealed wounds,** stop.
Take a **deep breath.**
Ask: "Is this my trauma talking, or my truth?"

- 03 -

THE "ANCESTOR REWRITE" LETTER

Write a **letter** to an ancestor who suffered. Tell them:
**"I will not let your story be repeated.
I carry your strength, not your pain."**

THE "ANCESTOR REWRITE" LETTER

Write a letter to an ancestor who suffered. Tell them:
"I will not let your story be repeated. I carry your strength, not your pain."

MINDSET SHIFTS TO FREE YOURSELF FROM GENERATIONAL CHAINS

- 01 -

I DO NOT HAVE TO LIVE THE SAME LIFE AS MY ANCESTORS.

I can choose differently.

- 02 -

I AM NOT RESPONSIBLE FOR CARRYING THEIR PAIN, ONLY FOR HEALING MY OWN.

- 03 -

THE FACT THAT I SEE THE CYCLE MEANS I HAVE THE POWER TO BREAK IT.

- 04 -

I WILL NOT PASS THIS TRAUMA ON.

The generations after me will know love, not survival.

PRACTICAL STEPS TO STOP PASSING DOWN THE PAIN

- 01 -

RECOGNIZE THE PATTERNS

What cycles do you see in your family? Abuse, addiction, emotional neglect, silence? Awareness is the first step to **breaking them.**

- 02 -

SET BOUNDARIES (EVEN WHEN IT HURTS)

Sometimes, **healing means saying "no" to people who raised you. That is not betrayal. That is self-preservation.**

- 03 -

LEARN NEW RELATIONSHIP MODELS

If you grew up in **chaos, healthy love might feel "boring" at first.** Learn to recognize safety. Learn to trust calm.

- 04 -

THERAPY, SELF-WORK, AND UNLEARNING

Generational trauma **doesn't heal on its own.** It requires work, therapy, journaling, meditation, and mentorship.

REFLECTION QUESTIONS: TAKING YOUR POWER BACK

WHAT GENERATIONAL PATTERNS HAVE BEEN PASSED DOWN IN YOUR FAMILY?

HOW CAN YOU ACTIVELY MAKE SURE THE NEXT GENERATION DOESN'T CARRY THIS PAIN FORWARD?

REFLECTION QUESTIONS: TAKING YOUR POWER BACK

WHAT BELIEFS ABOUT LOVE, TRUST, OR SELF-WORTH DID YOU INHERIT?
AND WHICH ONES NO LONGER SERVE YOU?

WHICH BELIEFS NO LONGER SERVE YOU?

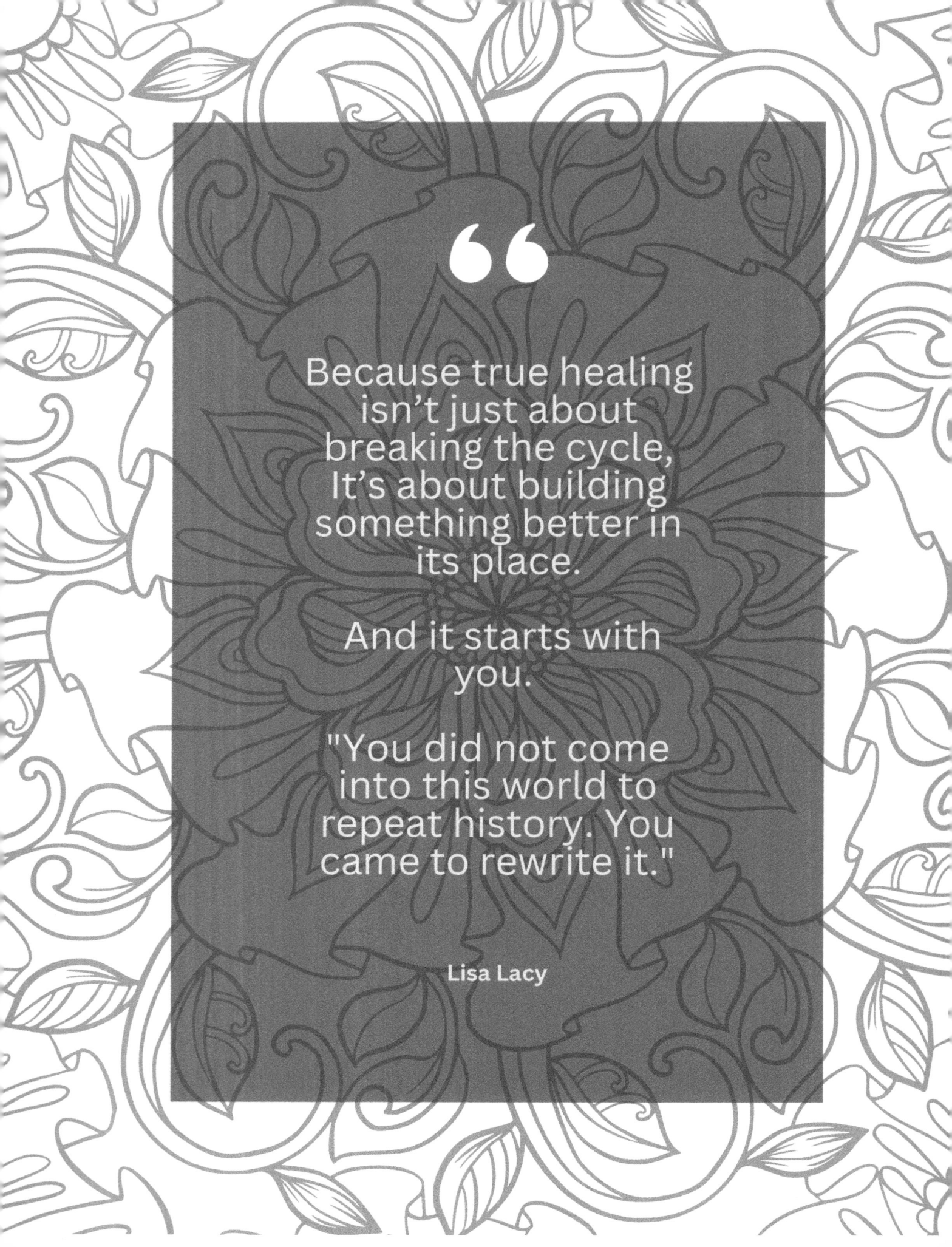

"

Because true healing isn't just about breaking the cycle, It's about building something better in its place.

And it starts with you.

"You did not come into this world to repeat history. You came to rewrite it."

Lisa Lacy

CHAPTER

09

SAYING F'OFF TO TRAUMA BONDS & CODEPENDENCY - LEARNING TO LOVE WITHOUT CHAINS

The Addictive Nature of Pain

Some people mistake **trauma bonds for love. I know, because I did.**

For most of my life, I thought love meant **survival together,** clinging to each other through pain, **weathering every storm,** and never leaving, **no matter how much it hurt.**

I thought that if **I suffered for someone,** stayed through the chaos, and **tolerated just a little more,** it meant I was **loyal.** For me, **attachment was love.** But **trauma bonds aren't love. They are addictions,** ones that feed off the wounds of your past, and make **you mistake pain for passion, intensity for intimacy, and chaos for connection.**

I stayed in relationships where I was **not valued, respected, or loved in the way I deserved,** but I convinced myself that because I felt **something so deeply,** it had to mean something **real.**

- I ignored the **red flags.**
- I made **excuses for the manipulation.**
- I let myself be **drained, controlled, abandoned, and discarded,** over and over again.

When I **finally woke up** and I saw what I had been **trapped in,** I had to ask myself: **Why do I keep choosing this?**

Because here's the **hard truth:**

- **I was never really choosing them.**
- I was **choosing familiar pain.**
- I was **choosing the version of love I was conditioned to accept.**

And if **I wanted something different,** I had to **break free.**

UNDERSTANDING TRAUMA BONDS (WHY WE STAY IN TOXIC LOVE)

A trauma bond isn't just an unhealthy relationship.

It's a **cycle of addiction** to emotional highs and lows, where love is **intertwined with pain. Leaving feels impossible;** and you believe **suffering is the price you have to pay for connection.**

The cycle is always the same:

- **Love Bombing** – They make you **feel seen, chosen, special. The intensity is intoxicating.**
- **Manipulation & Erosion** – Slowly, they **chip away at your self-worth. They guilt-trip, gaslight, or devalue you,** but just enough to make you **question yourself.**
- **The "Fix" (Intermittent Reinforcement)** – When you start pulling away, they **throw you just enough kindness, love, and hope to keep you hooked.**
- **Repeat the Cycle** – You stay, believing the **love is still there.** That if you **try hard enough, endure just a little more,** things will get better.

But they don't. Trauma bonds keep you in **survival mode,** triggering the same **fight-or-flight response** as **actual danger.** They keep you **chasing the "good moments"** while **drowning in the bad.** And the worst part? When you **finally try to leave,** it feels like **withdrawal,** because you've been **conditioned to crave the chaos.**

HOW CODEPENDENCY KEEPS YOU TRAPPED

Trauma bonds and codependency go hand in hand.

Where **trauma bonding is the cycle, codependency is the mindset** that keeps you **locked inside it.** I was **codependent** for most of my life.

I thought:
- **If I love them enough, they will change.**
- **If I just prove my worth, they won't leave.**
- **If I fix their pain, they will finally see me.**

I **made myself small** so others could feel **big;** and poured from an empty cup, hoping they'd **give me just a drop in return.** I stayed in **places I had outgrown** because I didn't know **who I was without them.** And the truth is, I wasn't **staying for love.**

I was **staying because of fear.**
- **Fear of being alone.**
- **Fear of being unloved.**
- **Fear of facing myself without someone else to distract me.**

Because when you're **codependent,** your **identity is built around other people.** And when they leave, you don't just **lose them, you lose yourself.**

THE BREAKING POINT (WHEN I FINALLY LET GO)

For years, I believed I could fix people.
I attracted **broken souls,** people who **needed saving;** and people who **needed my energy** more than they **valued my presence.**
I gave and gave and gave, **until there was nothing left of me.**
And then, one day, I woke up and realized:
This is not love. This is self-abandonment.
I was so afraid of **losing them** that I had **lost myself in the process.**

And that was the day I decided:
F'OFF.

- **F'OFF** to trauma bonds.
- **F'OFF** to people who only loved me when I was convenient.
- **F'OFF** to the version of me that accepted crumbs and called it love.

I wasn't going to **keep repeating my past.**
I was done **mistaking suffering for loyalty.**
And I was finally **ready to heal.**

MASTERING THE F'OFF FRAMEWORK TO BREAK TRAUMA BONDS

F – FACE THE TRUTH

Love should never feel like survival. Face it. Name it. **Own your truth.**
Action Step: Write down **one time** you confused **pain for love.**
What made you believe that **staying meant loyalty?**

MASTERING THE F'OFF FRAMEWORK TO BREAK TRAUMA BONDS

O – OWN YOUR BOUNDARIES

Walking away is not abandonment. It is self-respect.
Action Step: Set a **clear boundary** with yourself:
"I will not mistake suffering for connection."
"I will not tolerate toxic love in the name of loyalty."

F – FULLY CHOOSE YOURSELF

You do not need to suffer to prove you are worthy.
Action Step: Say this out loud: **"I am worthy of love that does not hurt. I do not have to earn it through suffering."**

F – FEARLESSLY TAKE ACTION

Healing from trauma bonds is not passive. It requires action.
Action Step: Take one concrete step today, whether it's **blocking a toxic ex, cutting ties with someone who drains you, or choosing to be alone rather than settling.**

SMALL RITUALS TO BREAK TRAUMA BONDS & CODEPENDENCY

- 01 -

THE "REALITY CHECK" JOURNAL

Every time you feel the urge to **go back to a toxic person,** write down all the times they **hurt you, made you feel small, or drained your energy.**

- 02 -

THE "SELF-TRUST" PRACTICE

Every day, ask yourself:
"What do I need today?"
Then, actually **give it to yourself, without waiting for someone else to.**

- 03 -

MIRROR WORK FOR SELF-WORTH

Stand in front of the mirror and say:
**"I am not responsible for fixing others.
I am worthy of love that does not hurt."**

THE REALITY CHECK

Every time you feel the urge to go back to a toxic person, **write down all the times they hurt you,** made you feel small, or drained your energy.

MINDSET SHIFTS TO BREAK FREE

- O1 -

LOVE SHOULD NEVER FEEL LIKE SURVIVAL.

- O2 -

**I DO NOT NEED TO SUFFER TO PROVE
I AM WORTHY.**

- O3 -

IF I HAVE TO BEG FOR LOVE, IT ISN'T LOVE.

- O4 -

**WALKING AWAY IS NOT ABANDONMENT.
IT IS SELF-RESPECT.**

PRACTICAL STEPS TO DETACH & REBUILD YOUR LIFE

- O1 -

GO NO CONTACT
(OR AT LEAST REDUCE EXPOSURE)

Block them, delete their number, create distance.

- O2 -

STOP EXPLAINING YOURSELF

You do not owe toxic people **closure.**

- O3 -

START A "ME FIRST" ERA

Reclaim your hobbies, goals, and dreams.

- O4 -

LEARN WHAT HEALTHY LOVE FEELS LIKE

At first, **stability may feel "boring" compared to the chaos** you're used to. **Trust the calm.**

REFLECTION QUESTIONS: BREAKING THE CHAINS

WHEN DID YOU MISTAKE PAIN FOR LOVE?

_____

_____

_____

_____

_____

_____

_____

_____

WHAT PATTERNS HAVE REPEATED IN YOUR RELATIONSHIPS?

_____

_____

_____

_____

_____

_____

_____

_____

REFLECTION QUESTIONS: BREAKING THE CHAINS

WHAT DOES A HEALTHY RELATIONSHIP LOOK LIKE TO YOU, AND HAVE YOU EVER EXPERIENCED ONE?

IF YOU WEREN'T AFRAID OF BEING ALONE, WHO WOULD YOU STOP CHASING?

BECAUSE REAL LOVE DOESN'T CHAIN YOU.
IT SETS YOU FREE.

YOU DON'T HEAL BY GOING BACK TO WHAT
BROKE YOU. YOU HEAL BY LEARNING TO LOVE
YOURSELF MORE THAN THE NEED TO BE CHOSEN.

Lisa Lacy

CHAPTER
10

SAYING F'OFF TO HIGH EXPECTATIONS OF MYSELF & LOW EXPECTATIONS OF EVERYONE ELSE

The Weight of Impossible Standards

I don't remember the exact moment I started expecting **the absolute most from myself** and **the bare minimum** from everyone else, but I do remember **what it felt like.** It felt like **carrying the weight of the world** while watching others glide through life, **unbothered and unburdened.**

It felt like **constantly proving myself, earning my place, doing more, being more,** and then accepting **crumbs** from the people around me.
For years, I lived by an **unspoken rule:**
Be everything to everyone. Expect nothing in return.
At first, it didn't even feel like a **choice;** it felt like **survival.**

- I had been **let down so many times** that I stopped expecting much from people.
- I had been **disappointed so often** that I learned to just **handle everything myself.**
- I had been **abandoned enough** to believe that if I wasn't **constantly overperforming,** I would be **forgotten.**

So, I made myself indispensable.
- I worked harder than everyone else.
- I carried the emotional weight in my relationships.
- I handled problems before they even became problems.
- I never asked for help because I didn't trust anyone to actually show up.

And for years, I called it **strength.**
But here's what **no one tells you about being the strong one:**
It's a lonely **F'OFF** place to be.

WHERE IT STARTED: THE ORIGIN OF SELF-IMPOSED PRESSURE

This pattern didn't come from nowhere.

Like so many of my struggles, **it was rooted in my past.**
I grew up watching people **disappoint me.**
I learned **young** that if I didn't **take care of myself,** no one else would.

I saw it when **my father, who was hardened by prison fighting demons that were never there. I saw it when my mother, still a child herself, had no choice but to survive instead of nurture.** I saw it when I had to **grow up too fast,** when there was **no one to lean on.**

I realized that **if I didn't figure things out myself, no one else would; so, I did.**

I BUILT AN IDENTITY AROUND BEING THE ONE WHO COULD HANDLE IT ALL.

- 01 -

IN RELATIONSHIPS, I BECAME THE CARETAKER

Anticipating needs, smoothing over conflicts, adjusting myself to make others comfortable. Because deep down,
I believed love had to be earned.

- 02 -

IN WORK, I BECAME THE OVERACHIEVER

I couldn't just be **good**. I had to be **the best**.
If I wasn't constantly excelling, I felt like I was **failing**.

- 03 -

IN FRIENDSHIPS, I BECAME THE PROBLEM-SOLVER

People came to me with their issues, and **I gladly took them on,** never expecting the same level of care in return.

- 04 -

IN MY OWN MIND, I BECAME MY HARSHEST CRITIC

No matter **how much I did,** it never felt like **enough.**

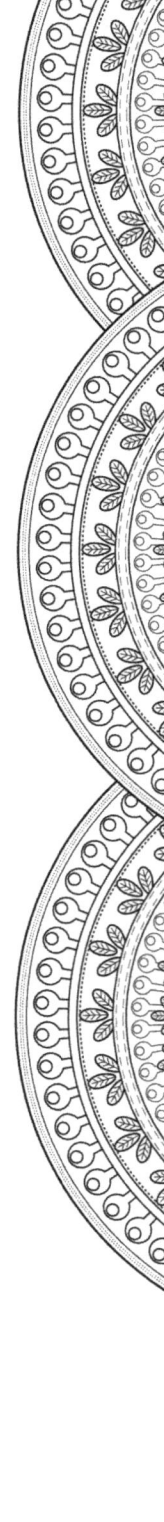

AT THE SAME TIME, I STARTED LOWERING MY EXPECTATIONS OF OTHERS.

Because if you don't expect much, you can't be disappointed, right?

- **I gave 110%** while accepting 10% in return.
- **I showed up fully** while making excuses for people who barely tried.
- **I demanded excellence from myself** while letting others skate by.

I made it **so easy for people to do nothing,** and then **I resented them for it.**

But the truth? I had trained them that way.
I had taught them that **I would always show up**, that I didn't need anything that I would carry the weight while they got to be light.
And eventually, **I broke.**

THE BREAKING POINT: WHEN I FINALLY SAID "ENOUGH"

There wasn't one single breaking point.

There were **a thousand small moments,** tiny cracks in the foundation of my life. Moments when I found myself **picking up the slack, doing the emotional labor,** carrying **more than my fair share,** while others **coasted.** Moments when I realized I was **draining myself to keep relationships alive that should have died long ago.** Moments when I caught myself **expecting nothing from others,** just so **I wouldn't have to feel the sting of disappointment.**

And then, one day, I saw it **clearly.**

- I was **operating at 200%** while expecting the **world to give me 20%.**
- I was holding myself to an **impossible standard** while **letting everyone else off the hook.**
- I was **overperforming, overgiving, and overextending** while **making excuses** for the people who refused to meet me halfway.

And for what?
So I could say I was strong, prove I was capable?
So I could avoid the discomfort of holding people accountable?
That was the day I chose myself; that was the day I decided: **F'OFF.**

- **F'OFF** to the self-imposed pressure that made me feel like I had to be perfect.
- **F'OFF** to the belief that my worth was tied to my productivity.
- **F'OFF** to the low expectations that kept me stuck in one-sided relationships.

I wasn't going to keep **carrying more than my share,** and I wasn't going to **accept less than I deserved.**

MASTERING THE F'OFF FRAMEWORK TO RESET EXPECTATIONS

F – FACE THE TRUTH

Overworking is not strength, it's self-neglect. Face it. Name it. Own your truth.
Action Step: Write down one area of your life where you expect more from yourself than you do from others. Ask: **Why do I accept this imbalance?**

MASTERING THE F'OFF FRAMEWORK TO RESET EXPECTATIONS

O – OWN YOUR BOUNDARIES

Expecting effort, accountability, and respect is not "asking for too much."
Action Step: The next time someone **does the bare minimum**, challenge yourself:
Do I call them out? Or do I let it slide (again)?

_____

_____

_____

_____

_____

_____

_____

F – FULLY CHOOSE YOURSELF

You deserve rest, grace, and support just like everyone else.
Action Step: Say this out loud:
"I am not superhuman. I will not carry more than my fair share."

F – FEARLESSLY TAKE ACTION

Change starts when you decide to stop tolerating imbalance.
Action Step: Step back from one responsibility this week and see who steps up.

SMALL RITUALS TO STOP OVERWORKING & UNDER-EXPECTING

- 01 -

THE "IS THIS FAIR?" CHECK-IN

Every time you feel yourself **taking on too much,** ask:
"Would I expect someone else to handle all of this?"

- 02 -

THE "WOULD I ACCEPT THIS FOR SOMEONE I LOVE?" TEST

If a friend were in your situation,
would you tell them to **accept what you're accepting?**

- 03 -

THE "STEP BACK" CHALLENGE

Once a week, **do not be the one who fixes, organizes, or carries everything. See who steps up, and who disappears.**

MINDSET SHIFTS TO BREAK FREE FROM THE DOUBLE STANDARD

- 01 -

I AM NOT SUPERHUMAN.

I deserve rest, grace, and support, just like everyone else.

- 02 -

IF PEOPLE DISAPPOINT ME, THAT'S ON THEM.

I do not need to lower my standards to accommodate them.

- 03 -

I DO NOT NEED TO EARN MY WORTH BY OVER-PERFORMING.

- 04 -

RESTING IS PRODUCTIVE.

I am enough even when I do nothing.

REFLECTION QUESTIONS: RECLAIMING BALANCE

WHERE IN MY LIFE DO I HOLD MYSELF TO IMPOSSIBLE STANDARDS?

WHERE DO I LET OTHERS GET AWAY WITH DOING LESS THAN THEY SHOULD?

REFLECTION QUESTIONS: RECLAIMING BALANCE

WHAT WOULD MY LIFE LOOK LIKE IF I STOPPED OVER-GIVING AND STARTED EXPECTING MORE?

HOW CAN I START HONORING MY OWN LIMITS WITHOUT GUILT?

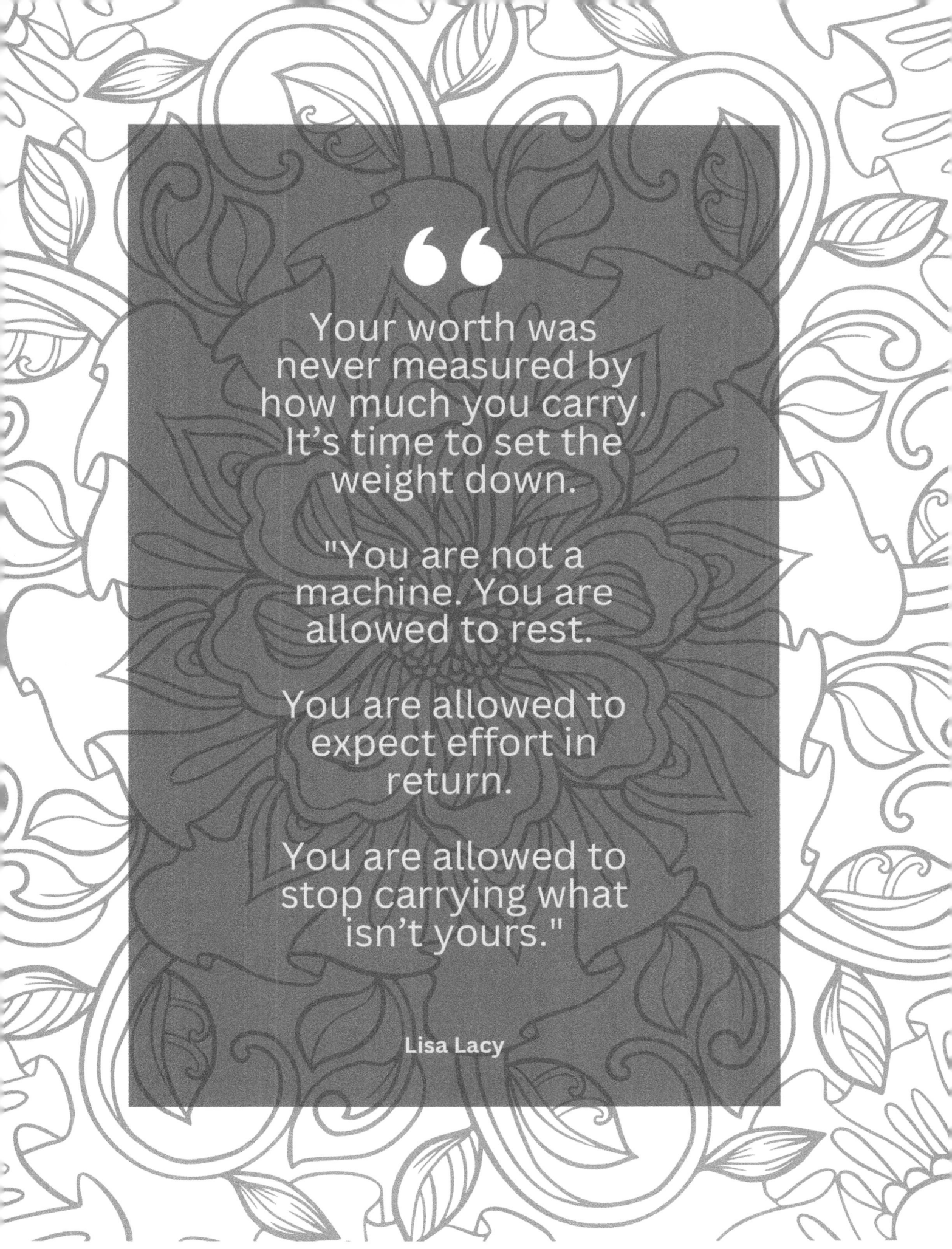

"

Your worth was
never measured by
how much you carry.
It's time to set the
weight down.

"You are not a
machine. You are
allowed to rest.

You are allowed to
expect effort in
return.

You are allowed to
stop carrying what
isn't yours."

Lisa Lacy

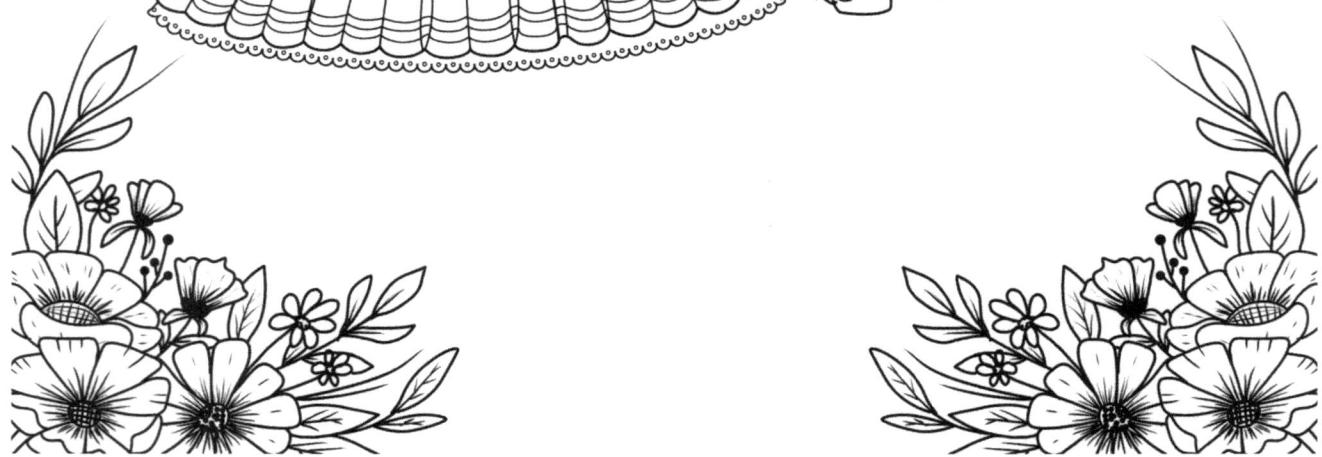

CHAPTER

11

SAYING F'OFF TO SURVIVAL MODE, CHOOSING JOY & BUILDING A LIFE YOU LOVE

Living in Constant Survival Mode

For most of my life, I wasn't really **living,** I was **surviving.**

- Waking up every day with my body still clenched from yesterday's battles.
- Bracing for the next crisis before the last one had even ended.
- Exhausted but unable to rest because my nervous system only knew one setting: high alert.

For years, I didn't **dream, plan, or imagine something better.**
Because when you've spent your **whole life in survival mode, your** trauma will convince you **that joy is a luxury you can't afford.**

TRAUMA TOLD ME:

- **"Stay ready. The worst is always just around the corner."**
- **"If you relax, you'll lose control."**
- **"You don't deserve happiness, only survival."**

And I **believed it.**
Because when you've lived through **mental illness, addiction, trauma, and a body that has betrayed you more times than you can count,** it's hard to believe in anything beyond **just making it through the day.** But one day, I realized: **F'OFF to this.**

I had fought **too hard,** survived **too much,** and rebuilt myself **too many times** to settle for a life that was just about **making it through.** I didn't just want to **survive.** I wanted to **live.**
I wanted **joy, peace, passion, adventure.**
I wanted to wake up in the morning with **something to look forward to,** something **bigger than just surviving the day.** So, I made a choice.
I said **F'OFF to survival mode.**
And I said **YES** to building a life that actually made me **excited to be alive.**

BREAKING THE ADDICTION TO STRUGGLE

Struggle becomes familiar when you've lived in **survival mode for so long. It's the default setting your brain returns to.**

Because at some point, I started believing that **if life wasn't hard, if I wasn't fighting for every breath, every ounce of peace, every scrap of stability, then I wasn't really earning it.**

The idea that I could just **have good things without suffering first?**
That felt **wrong.** So even after I got out of my worst situations, started recovering, left the people and places that hurt me, and found peace, I would still **subconsciously seek out struggle** because **struggle felt comfortable.**

JOY?
THAT FELT SUSPICIOUS.

- If I was happy, something bad was coming.
- If things were good, it meant they wouldn't last.
- If I let myself **relax,** I would lose everything I had fought for.

And that's when I realized:
I wasn't afraid of struggle; I was **afraid of peace,** because **I had never known a life where peace wasn't temporary.** But I was ready to **change that.**

THE MOMENT I CHOSE JOY

There wasn't a **single, dramatic moment** where everything clicked into place. It was a series of **small choices.**

- **Moments** where I caught myself **bracing for a fight that wasn't coming,** and **told myself to breathe instead.**
- **There were times** when I almost **sabotaged something amazing, because I was afraid of losing it,** before reminding myself that **I deserved good things, too.**
- **Times** when **I let myself enjoy something without questioning it.**

Slowly, **I stopped chasing struggle and started choosing ease.**
Instead of **waiting for permission** to enjoy my life, **I gave myself permission.**
Instead of **preparing for the worst,** I began to **expect something better.**
Instead of saying "I don't know if **I deserve this,"** I started saying "I **am allowed** to have this." And little by little, **my life changed.**
Because when you finally **start believing that joy is your birthright,** not just a rare accident, you **start building a life that reflects that truth.**

MASTERING THE F'OFF FRAMEWORK TO RESET EXPECTATIONS

F – FACE THE TRUTH

Face the Truth: You do not have to fight for everything in life. Some things can come with ease. Face it. Name it. **Own your truth.**

Action Step: Write down **one way** you make your life harder than it needs to be.

Ask yourself: "What if I chose ease instead, and how would that look?"

MASTERING THE F'OFF FRAMEWORK TO RESET EXPECTATIONS

O – OWN YOUR BOUNDARIES

Joy is not selfish. It is necessary. Action Step: Set a joy boundary, protect time in your day for something that brings you happiness, and **don't let guilt take it away.**

F – FULLY CHOOSE YOURSELF

You do not have to earn joy. You are worthy of it just as you are. Action Step: Say this out loud: **"I am not just here to survive. I am here to LIVE."**

F – FEARLESSLY TAKE ACTION

Joy is not passive. You have to choose it. Action Step: Take **one concrete step** toward something that excites you, whether it's **starting a passion project, planning a trip, or just allowing yourself to slow down without guilt.**

SMALL RITUALS TO SHIFT FROM SURVIVAL MODE TO JOY

- 01 -

THE "WHAT IF IT GOES RIGHT?"

Practice – Every time my brain tells me "This won't last" or "Something bad will happen", I pause and ask:
"What if this time, everything goes right?"
Because **joy deserves** as much of my imagination as fear does.

- 02 -

THE "EASE OVER EFFORT" CHECK-IN

Every time I catch myself taking the hardest possible path
(because I think I have to earn happiness),
I ask: **"Is there an easier way?"**
And **I choose ease** instead of unnecessary struggle.

- 03 -

THE "JOY FIRST" RULE

I do **one small thing every day** that brings me **joy,** even if it feels unproductive. **A song, a walk or a deep breath** in the sun
I remind myself that **joy** is not a reward, it's a **necessity.**

MINDSET SHIFTS TO FULLY EMBRACE LIFE

- 01 -

I DO NOT HAVE TO EARN JOY.

I am worthy of it just as I am.

- 02 -

HAPPINESS IS NOT TEMPORARY.

I can create a life where it is the norm, not the exception.

- 03 -

I AM NOT DEFINED BY MY PAST STRUGGLES.

I am **allowed to evolve,** to heal, to experience peace.

- 04 -

LIFE IS NOT SOMETHING I HAVE TO FIGHT THROUGH

it is something I am **allowed to enjoy.**

PRACTICAL STEPS TO BUILD THE LIFE YOU ACTUALLY WANT

- 01 -

IDENTIFY YOUR "DREAM LIFE" (WITHOUT LIMITS)

If you could live **any life,** without fear, without struggle, what would it look like? Write it down. Make it real. Start taking steps toward it.

- 02 -

LET GO OF IDENTITIES THAT NO LONGER SERVE YOU

If you have **built your identity** around suffering, around struggle, around being the "strong one" release it. **You are more than what you have survived.**

- 03 -

MAKE SPACE FOR JOY

Start **prioritizing things that make you happy.** Not just in theory, but in action. **Build a schedule that reflects what you love.**

- 04 -

REDEFINE SUCCESS

Instead of **measuring your life** by how much you've survived, **start measuring it by how much you enjoy it.**

MY DREAM LIFE

If you could live any life, without fear, without struggle, what would it look like? Write it down. Make it real. Start taking steps toward it.

REFLECTION QUESTIONS: STEPPING INTO YOUR BEST LIFE

WHAT PARTS OF YOUR LIFE ARE STILL ROOTED IN SURVIVAL MODE?

WHEN WAS THE LAST TIME YOU FELT TRUE, UNFILTERED JOY?

REFLECTION QUESTIONS: STEPPING INTO YOUR BEST LIFE

WHAT FEARS KEEP YOU FROM FULLY EMBRACING HAPPINESS?

IF YOU LET GO OF STRUGGLE, WHAT WOULD YOUR LIFE LOOK LIKE?

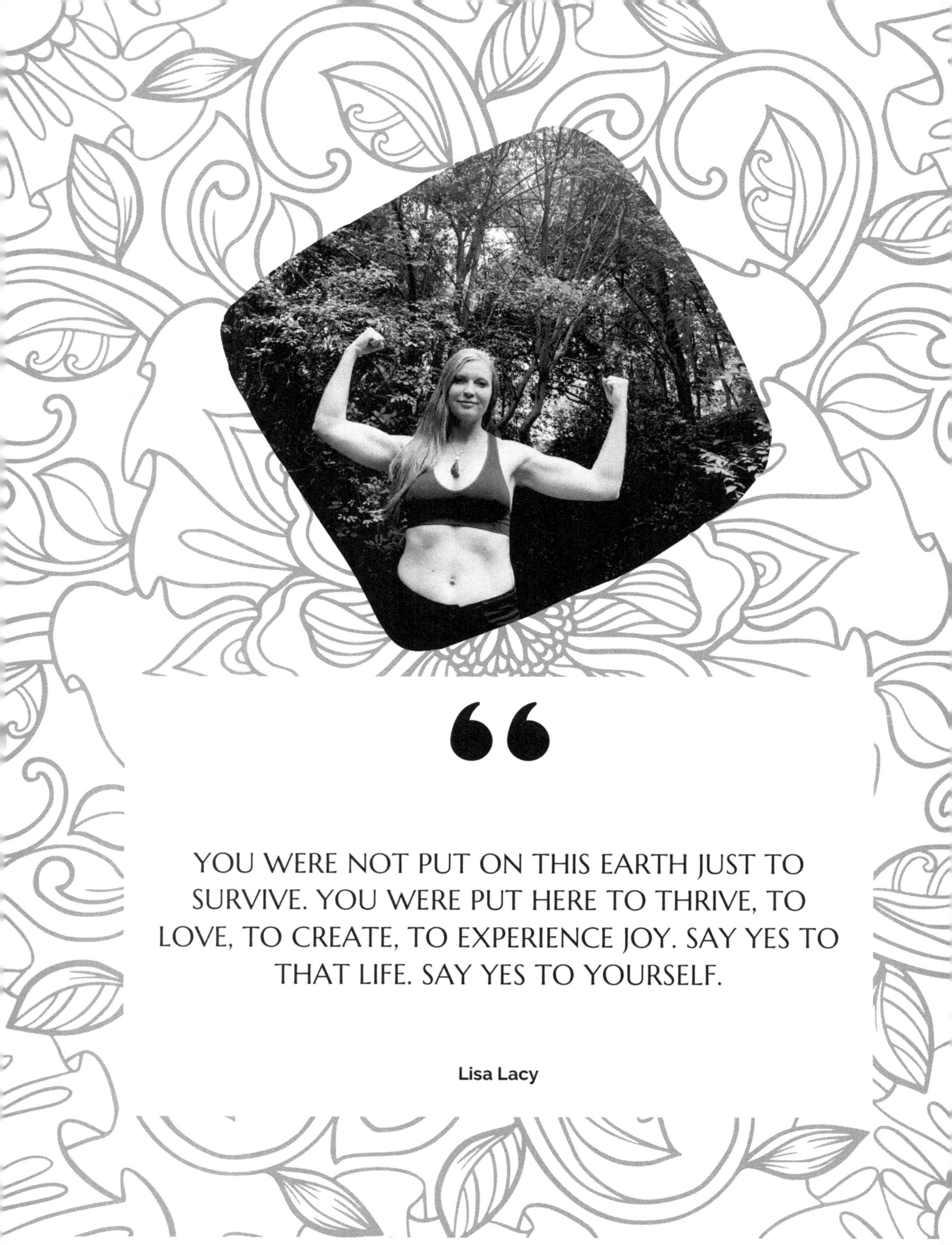

"

YOU WERE NOT PUT ON THIS EARTH JUST TO
SURVIVE. YOU WERE PUT HERE TO THRIVE, TO
LOVE, TO CREATE, TO EXPERIENCE JOY. SAY YES TO
THAT LIFE. SAY YES TO YOURSELF.

Lisa Lacy

CHAPTER

12

SAYING F'OFF TO NOT LOVING YOURSELF FIRST
THE POWER OF RADICAL SELF-LOVE

The Most Important Love Story You Will Ever Live

At the **end of everything,** after every **lesson, heartbreak, battle, survival, and rebuilding,** there is one truth that rises above them all:

You must love yourself first.
Not as a **cute idea.**
Not as a **surface-level affirmation.**
Not as something you say only when no one else is **giving you love.**
But as the **foundation of your entire existence.**
Because without **self-love,** nothing else truly works.
Without **self-love,** you will forever be seeking something outside of yourself to **make you feel whole.**

Without **self-love,** you will keep accepting less, giving too much, staying too long, shrinking too small. And I did all of that.

For years. Decades. A **lifetime** before I finally said: **Enough!**

Because if I had to spend the rest of my life with anyone, it would be **me.**
And I refused to live that life, being at war with the one person who would never leave me.
So I chose me. And that decision **changed everything.**

WHY WE WERE TAUGHT TO LOVE OTHERS FIRST (AND WHY THAT'S BULLSHIT)

The world teaches us that loving ourselves is selfish.

We are told that to be **a good person, a good friend, a good partner, or a good parent,** we must prioritize the needs of others. We are taught that **our worth** is measured by how much we **give, sacrifice, and endure.**
But you know what I've learned? That is the **biggest lie we've ever been told.**
Because when you **love yourself first,** you actually have more to give, not less.
When you pour from an overflowing cup, you give out of joy, not obligation.
Because when you **love yourself deeply,** you **don't tolerate relationships where that love is not returned.** This is **not selfish.** It is **survival.**

Because when you put everyone else above yourself, this is what happens:

- **You overgive** until you are empty.
- **You accept love that is beneath you** because you believe that's all you deserve.
- **You contort yourself** into versions that please others but suffocate you.
- **You never actually get to know who you are** because your existence revolves around others.

AND THE COST?

- Your **peace.**
- Your **joy.**
- Your **truth.**
- Your **life.**

So, I say this with **absolute certainty: F'OFF** to that.

- **F'OFF** to the conditioning that told you to put yourself last.
- **F'OFF** to the guilt that makes you feel selfish for choosing yourself.
- **F'OFF** to the belief that you must love others before you love yourself.

Because the truth is, **you will never truly know love until you first give it to yourself.**

THE JOURNEY TO LOVING MYSELF FIRST

I didn't wake up one day suddenly full of self-love.

It was **a process.** A long, messy undoing. Because first, I had to unlearn everything I had been taught about love. I had to realize that **love** is not self-abandonment. If I had to betray myself to keep someone, that wasn't love; that was fear.

- **Love is not overgiving.** If I had to give and give without receiving, that wasn't love, that was depletion.
- **Love is not earned.** If I had to prove my worth to be loved, that wasn't love, that was validation-seeking.
- **Love should** never require me to become less of who I am.

And after unlearning? I had to rebuild.

I HAD TO LEARN HOW TO:

- O1 -

SPEAK TO MYSELF KINDLY AFTER YEARS OF TEARING MYSELF DOWN.

- O2 -

HONOR MY NEEDS AFTER A LIFETIME OF IGNORING THEM.

- O3 -

SET BOUNDARIES AFTER YEARS OF LETTING THEM BE CROSSED.

- O4 -

BELIEVE THAT I WAS WORTHY OF GOOD LOVE AFTER ACCEPTING CRUMBS FOR SO LONG.

AND THE BIGGEST LESSON?

I had to learn that loving myself was not conditional.

Not based on how **productive** I was.
Not based on how **desirable** I was.
Not based on whether **someone else loved me back.**
But simply **because I existed.**
Because **I am here.**
Because **I have breath in my lungs.**
Because **I deserve love,** not later, not when I was 'better,' not when I had 'earned it.'
Right now. **Exactly as I am.**

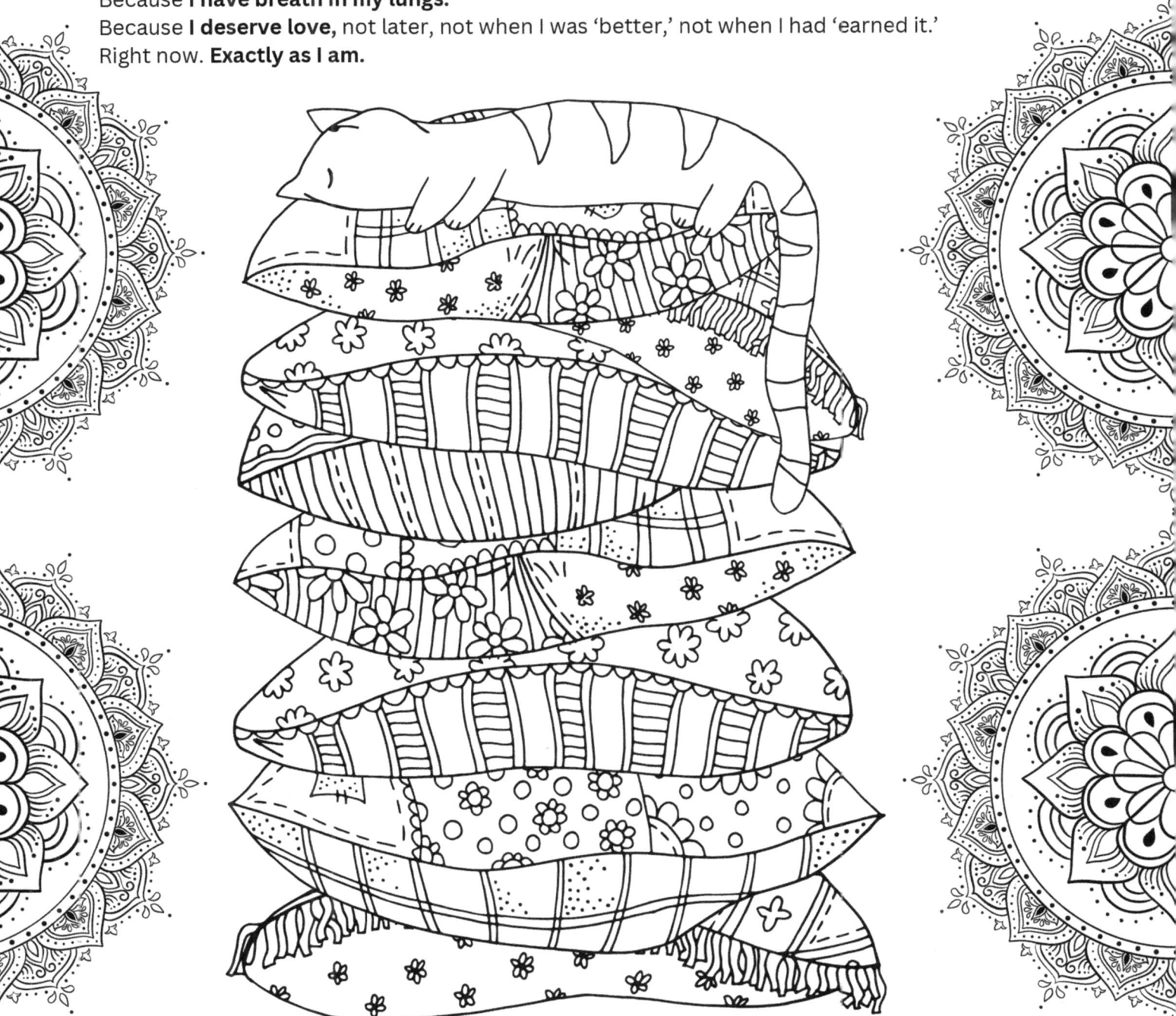

MASTERING THE F'OFF FRAMEWORK TO RESET EXPECTATIONS

F – FACE THE TRUTH

If you don't love yourself, you will accept love that isn't real.
Face it. Name it. Own your truth.
Action Step: Write down one way you have abandoned yourself in the name of love.
Ask: **"What would it look like to choose myself instead?"**

MASTERING THE F'OFF FRAMEWORK TO RESET EXPECTATIONS

O – OWN YOUR BOUNDARIES

You set the standard for how others love you. Do not lower it.
Action Step: Identify **one relationship** where your self-love is compromised.
Set a boundary and enforce it without apology.

_____

_____

_____

_____

_____

_____

_____

F – FULLY CHOOSE YOURSELF

Your relationship with yourself is the most important one you will ever have. Action Step: Say this out loud:
"I am my own greatest love story. I will love myself first, always."

F – FEARLESSLY TAKE ACTION

Self-love is not passive. It requires action.
Action Step: Take one concrete **step toward building a life that reflects self-love,** whether it's saying no, **putting yourself first, or letting go** of toxic people.

SMALL RITUALS TO SHIFT FROM SURVIVAL MODE TO JOY

- 01 -

THE "HOW WOULD I TREAT SOMEONE I LOVE?"

Practice – Every time I criticize myself, I pause and ask:
"Would I speak this way to someone I love?"
If the answer is no, **I reframe it with kindness.**

- 02 -

THE "LOVE LETTER TO MYSELF"

Ritual – I wrote a **letter to myself,** as if I were writing to
my dearest friend.
I remind myself of my strength, resilience, beauty, and worth.
I read it every time I forget.

- 03 -

THE "SELF-LOVE AS A STANDARD"

Rule – I refuse to accept relationships that do not meet the standard of
how I love myself.

THE LOVE LETTER

Write a letter to yourself, as if you were writing to your dearest friend.
Remind yourself of your strength, resilience, beauty, and worth.
Read it every time you forget.

MINDSET SHIFTS TO FULLY EMBRACE LIFE

- 01 -

**LOVING MYSELF IS NOT A REWARD.
IT IS MY FOUNDATION.**

- 02 -

**I DO NOT HAVE TO BE PERFECT TO
BE WORTHY OF LOVE.**

- 03 -

**THE WAY I LOVE MYSELF SETS THE STANDARD
FOR HOW OTHERS LOVE ME.**

- 04 -

I AM MY OWN GREATEST LOVE STORY.

FINAL REFLECTION QUESTIONS: YOUR SELF-LOVE JOURNEY

WHEN WAS THE LAST TIME YOU PUT YOURSELF FIRST, WITHOUT GUILT?

WHAT OLD BELIEFS ABOUT LOVE DO YOU NEED TO UNLEARN?

FINAL REFLECTION QUESTIONS: YOUR SELF-LOVE JOURNEY

IF YOU LOVED YOURSELF THE WAY YOU LOVE OTHERS, HOW WOULD YOUR LIFE CHANGE?

WHAT IS ONE WAY YOU CAN SHOW YOURSELF LOVE TODAY?

F'OFF MANIFESTO: SELF-LOVE EDITION

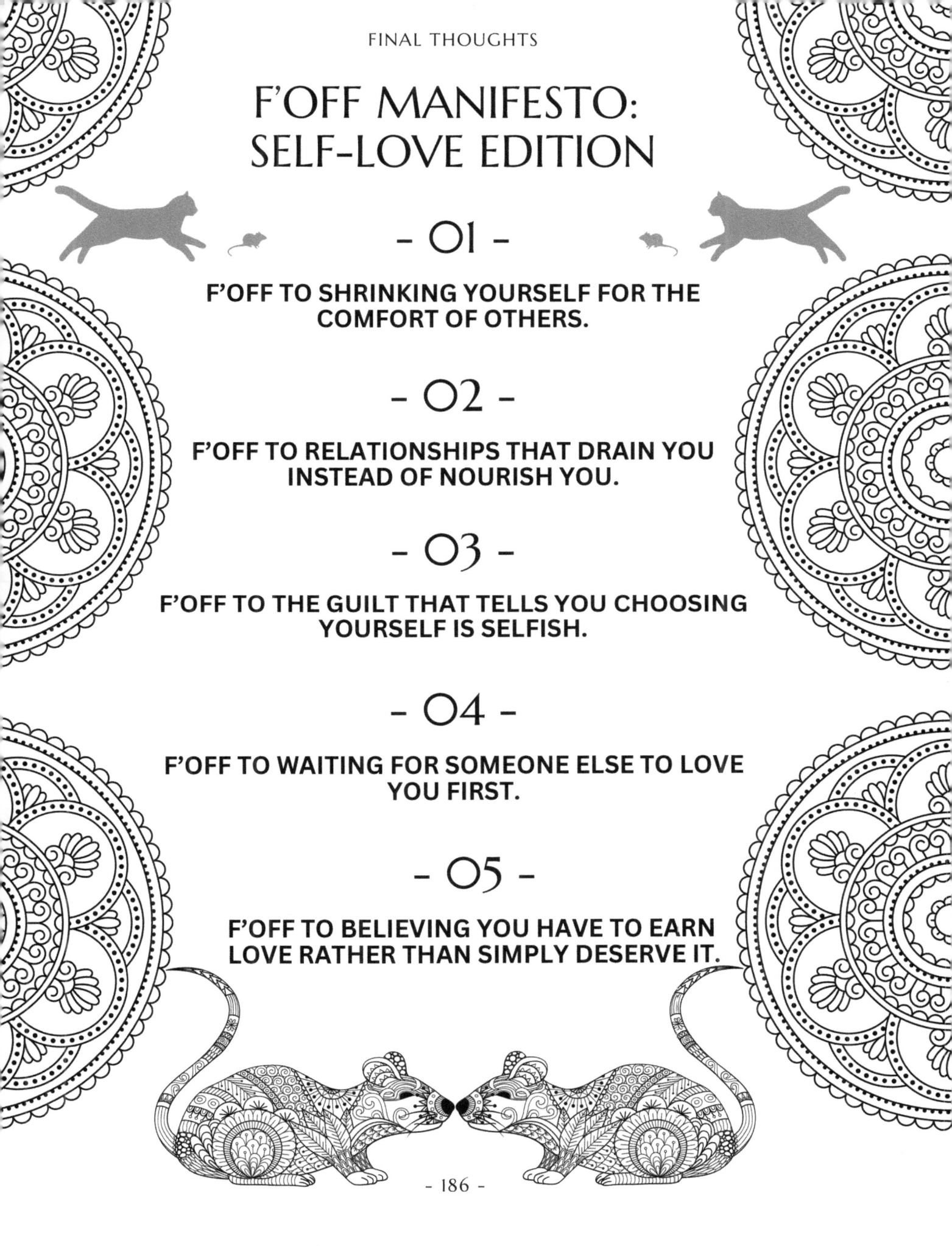

- 01 -

F'OFF TO SHRINKING YOURSELF FOR THE COMFORT OF OTHERS.

- 02 -

F'OFF TO RELATIONSHIPS THAT DRAIN YOU INSTEAD OF NOURISH YOU.

- 03 -

F'OFF TO THE GUILT THAT TELLS YOU CHOOSING YOURSELF IS SELFISH.

- 04 -

F'OFF TO WAITING FOR SOMEONE ELSE TO LOVE YOU FIRST.

- 05 -

F'OFF TO BELIEVING YOU HAVE TO EARN LOVE RATHER THAN SIMPLY DESERVE IT.

FINAL CLOSING THOUGHT: YOUR GREATEST LOVE STORY BEGINS NOW

At the **end of the day,** everything I have **learned,** everything I have **fought for,** everything I have **healed from,** it all comes down to **this:**

I **choose me.**

And if anything, or **anyone,** tries to **convince you otherwise?**

You already **know what to say.**

F'OFF.

FINAL CLOSING THOUGHT: YOUR GREATEST LOVE STORY BEGINS NOW

Stepping Fully into Your Savage Sovereignty

You made it. Through every chapter, exercise, and revelation, **you've peeled back** the layers of conditioning, **reclaimed your truth,** and **fortified your boundaries.** You've confronted the ghosts of doubt, **broken the chains** of inherited limitations, and stepped into the **unshakable force that is YOU.**

But this journey doesn't end here.

Sovereignty isn't a destination, it's a daily devotion. A practice. A way of breathing, moving, and existing in a world that often demands your submission. **Reclaiming your power** is not a one-time act; it is a **fierce,** ongoing **commitment to yourself.**

So, what now?

- Continue to **honor your "No"** as sacred and your "Yes" as sovereign.
- **Trust that your energy,** time, and presence are currency; **spend them wisely.**
- **Know** that your ancestors, your spirit, and **your intuition** will never lead you astray.
- And **above all, never apologize** for the space you take up in this world.

This is your power. This is your legacy. This is your F'Off energy in full force. Keep rising. Keep reclaiming. Keep roaring.
I'll see you on the path.
With sovereignty and fire.

Lisa Lacy

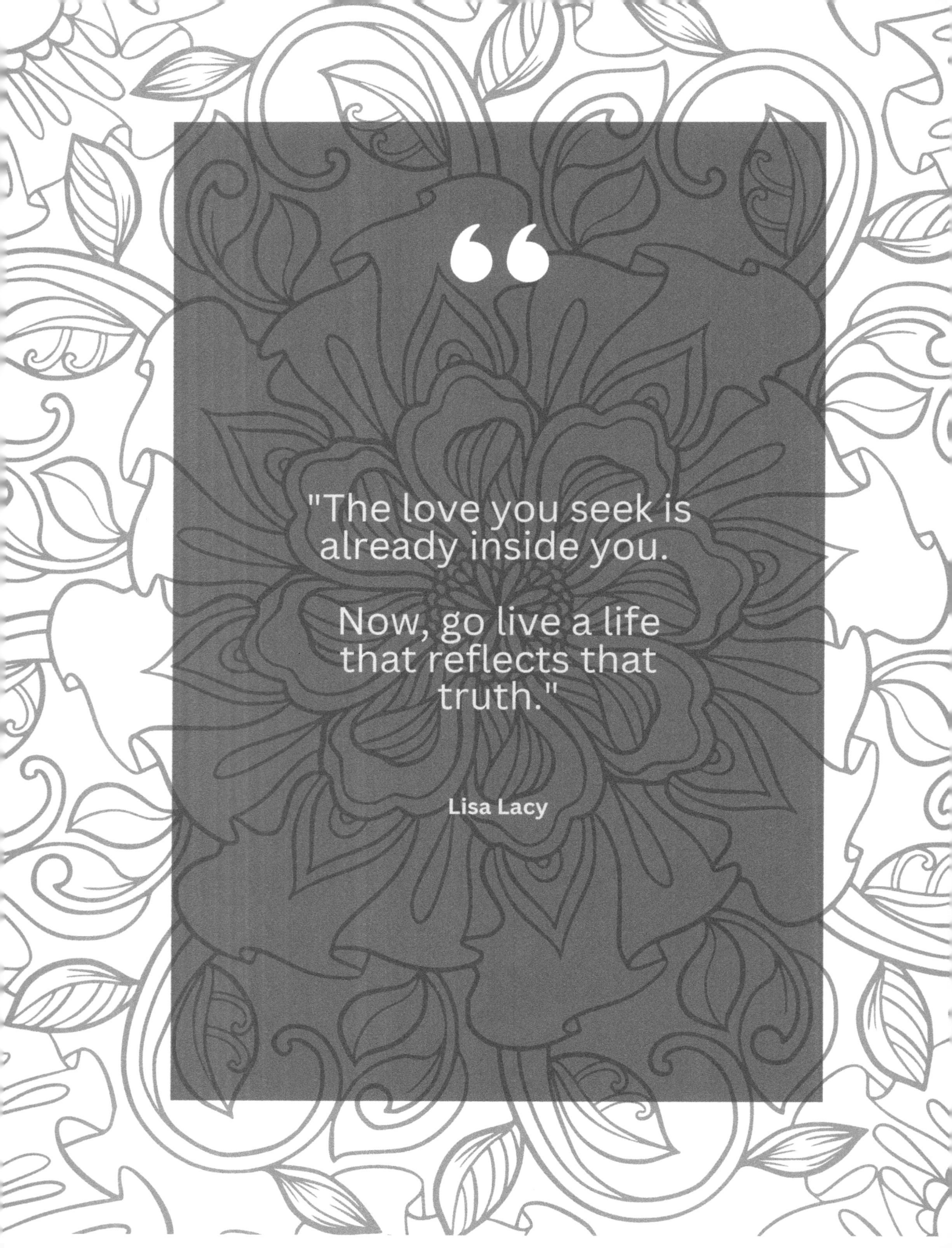

"

"The love you seek is already inside you.

Now, go live a life that reflects that truth."

Lisa Lacy